# GOOD FOOD FOR ALL

# GOOD FOOD FOR ALL

## Developing knowledge relationships between China and Australia

Editors

Bruno Mascitelli & Barry O'Mahony

Connor Court Publishing

Connor Court Publishing Pty Ltd



PO Box 224W
Ballarat VIC 3350
sales@connorcourt.com
www.connorcourt.com

ISBN: 9781925138399 (pbk.)

Cover design by Maria Giordano, photo taken from iStockphoto.com

Printed in Australia

# CONTENTS

# Acknowledgements

This book comprises a collection of essays which emanated from an important Australia China Council (ACC) sponsored event conducted in Wuhan, China, in November 2013. The editors of this book along with Dr. Jue Chen, all from Swinburne University of Technology, Melbourne, were the successful recipients of this award for a project involving a two day forum entitled 'Australia-China Food Knowledge Exchange'.

Organised as a joint exercise with our Chinese counterparts and co-hosts, Huazhong Agricultural University of Wuhan, the event brought together experts in diverse aspects of food in both China and Australia. We are most grateful to the Rector of Huazhong Agricultural University Professor Xiannong Zhang and especially to Vice President Chongguang Li who provided logistical support and encouraged a large Chinese delegation to take part.

We are equally thankful to Professor Ping who organised many of the Chinese speakers and brought academic and industry attendees to contribute to the event. The welcoming presentations from the Australian delegation included Mr. Jeff Turner, Senior Trade Commissioner for Austrade Chengdu (China) and Mr. Patrick Stringer from the Victorian Government based in Hong Kong. We are most thankful to both of these gentlemen for their participation and thoughtful comments made on the food relationship between Australia and China.

Over the two days of discussion participants engaged with important presentations on questions related to food supply, logistics, pricing, organic food, food security and other related topics. We are proud to include the program in the appendices of this book. The event was extremely successful in achieving its aims with an audience of over 300 participants listening to 10 speakers on the Australian side and an equal number on the Chinese side. This event has now resulted in the production of this collection of important essays as a testimony to this valuable exchange of knowledge and experience across the two nations.

The feedback from the two day event was so overwhelmingly positive that we felt a responsibility to provide some scholarly treatment of the event and invited experts and scholars to contribute to this book. We are especially thankful to our authors for having contributed to this event and ultimately producing the scholarly works contained in this book. It is a tribute to their expertise that the quality of the event is matched by the quality of their contributions and provides an indication of the vibrancy of our discussions in Wuhan. We offer a special thank you to the authors of each respective essay.

We are also mindful that without the award from the Australian Government through the ACC this important event would not have been possible. We are, therefore, extremely grateful to the ACC for their confidence in us and to Swinburne University of Technology for the conduct of this activity. We hope this book will offer evidence of this appreciation and present some insights into the quality event that took place in Wuhan in November 2013.

**Bruno Mascitelli and Barry O'Mahony**
**15 October 2014**

# Abbreviations

| | |
|---|---|
| BFA | Biological Farmers of Australia (now Australian Organic) |
| CSIRO | Commonwealth Scientific and Industrial Research Organisation |
| EU | European Union |
| FAO | Food and Agriculture organization of the United Nations |
| FDI | Foreign Direct Investment |
| FTA | Free Trade Agreement |
| G8 | Largest eight economies in the world |
| G20 | Largest 20 economies in the world |
| GATT | General Agreement on Tariffs and Trade |
| GDP | Gross Domestic Product |
| GFC | Global Financial Crisis |
| GM | Genetically Modified |
| GMO | Genetically Modified Organism |
| IFOAM | International Federation of Organic Agriculture Movements |
| IMF | International Monetary Fund |
| MDG | Millennium Development Goals |
| MNE | Multinational Enterprises |
| MoA | Ministry of Agriculture |
| NASAA | National Association for Sustainable Agriculture, Australia |
| OECD | Organisation for Economic Cooperation and Development |
| PRC | People's Republic of China |

| | |
|---|---|
| R&D | Research and Development |
| SOE | State Owned Enterprise |
| SME | Small Medium Enterprises |
| TNC | Trans National Corporation |
| UN | United Nations |
| UNHCR | United Nations High Commissioner for Refugees |
| UNCTAD | United Nations Conference on Trade and Development |
| USA | United States of America |
| USDA | United States Department of Agriculture |
| WFC | World Food Conference |
| WHO | World Health Organization |
| WTO | World Trade Organization |

# List of tables and figures

## Tables



## Figures

# Preface

## Tony Bilson

The remarkable and continued growth of the Chinese economy offers a future partnership for our two countries that will demand not just economic ties and exchanges but a dynamic program of cultural and intellectual exchange. While much has been made of a Chinese economic slowdown in the press we must focus on the fact that the Chinese economy will double in the next 10 years from what is an already high base. This economic change has been accompanied by a change in Chinese consumer patterns that offer long term opportunities to Australia.

*Good Food For All* offers an insight into many of the problems and opportunities intrinsic to these developments. Figures contained in the study will shock many Australians, if Crocodile Dundee thought he had a big knife he should see the Chinese version. In many ways it is the sheer size of the market that presents one of the biggest problems to food and wine producers and indeed our nation.

*Good Food For All* analyses the opportunities in food production and co-operation available to our two countries. The remarkable opportunity offered, of which the *Good Food For All* conference is a great example, is an exchange of ideas and culture provoked by mutual need. The cultural exchange is for me the most fascinating. While all cultures move along a path of continual change the last decade has seen exponential change in China, with Australia being dragged into accommodating these extraordinary phenomena. The growth of the Chinese interest in wine is matched by the Australian interest in Asian food. The growth of Chinese tourism, now in its infancy, will demand a greater cultural sensitivity from Australians while at the same time broadening Chinese cultural perspectives. China is already the largest source of in-bound tourism to Australia and is graduating from bus tours to individual visitations at a high rate. As well, 20 per cent of all Sydney real estate sales are now to Chinese purchasers.

In order to address this challenge Australia needs the focus and investment only Government can provide at this stage. Our governmental agencies are well versed in marketing major mining exports but less comfortable with cultural orientations. In contrast New Zealand has successfully negotiated the marketing of the national brand with fewer cultural and financial resources than Australia, investing seriously in promotion and service in China. Our promotional investment, by contrast, seems too diversified and un-coordinated. The opportunity for industrial promotions integrating wine, food and other cultural components seems obvious but, at this stage, un-attainable. Instead of simply participating in international trade events we should be initiating them. The sheer size of the market demands partnerships between Government, industry, academia and the arts.

The discussion that will be provoked by the analysis and insight contained in *Good Food For All* should provoke major policy discussions and widen the awareness of business leaders to the potential benefits of partnerships within China and in Australia.

The benefits of cultural exchanges can perhaps best be expressed in the Chinese mantra that one builds business through building friendships. It is difficult to understand market parameters and drivers and anticipate future trends without cultural insight. It is therefore incumbent on government, major financial institutions and industrial exporters to support culturally orientated promotions and exchange.

The work of Dr Geoff Raby has been particularly insightful in this field.

The initiative represented in *Good Food For All* through the collaboration of Swinburne University of Technology and Huazhong Agricultural University in Wuhan is a fine example of the dialogue needed to formulate policy and build a solid base of understanding and friendship between our two countries.

**Tony Bilson**
**Creative Director**
**China- Australia New Horizons**
**14 October 2014**

# Biographies of contributors

## Tony Bilson

Recognised as one of Australia's leading chefs, Tony Bilson's restaurants have been milestones in the advance of Australian gastronomy. He has promoted Australian food and wine internationally as guest chef in some of the world's most prestigious hotels in Manila, Singapore, Chicago, Dubai, Bali, Munich, Mumbai, Madras, Bangalore, Calcutta, Delhi; Hong Kong, New York, Tokyo and Beijing. He has published six books including his memoir, *Insatiable – My Life in the Kitchen*. He is a senior member of the Academic Board of *Le Cordon Bleu* Australia, an Honorary Life Member of the Australian Restaurant and Catering Association and a Committee member of the *Academie Culinaire de France*. In his present role as Creative Director of Australia-China New Horizons he is creating a series of integrated wine, food and art promotions in China.

## John Dalrymple

John Dalrymple is Professor of Operations Management in the Faculty of Business and Enterprise at Swinburne University of Technology. John holds an Honours degree from the University of Stirling and a PhD from the University of Strathclyde in Scotland. John migrated to Australia in 1997 to become the Founding Director of the Centre for Management Quality Research at RMIT University. His research over the past twenty years has been in the area of performance measurement and performance improvement in organisations, with a particular emphasis on small and medium-sized enterprises. He has led numerous research projects; predominantly in Melbourne's Northern suburbs a number of projects focused on the food processing industry. John demonstrated the portability of a comprehensive business review instrument from its European context to the Australian small business environment. This instrument is now widely used in Australia.

### Donald Feaver

Donald Feaver is a Professor of Law and Deputy Head of Research and Innovation at the Graduate School of Business & Law, at RMIT University, Australia. Donald is admitted to practice as an Attorney and Counsellor at Law of the Supreme Court of New York and the Supreme Court of Victoria. Donald's research focus at the moment includes international and multilateral regulation, transnational law and regulation and international economic law relating to international trade practices such as antidumping and countervailing law and policy.

### Mark Gibson

In his early years in the culinary arts, Marks's perspective was very focused on the pragmatic issues of the kitchen. After many years, and building on this grounding in the culinary arts, his focus shifted to take in the wider perspective of food's role, not only in his own life but within society in general. For Mark there was an elemental desire to understand more of the social, political and economic tectonics of food culture. As a result of this process Mark found himself asking many difficult questions as well as challenging many widely accepted assumptions about humanities relationship with food. Not surprisingly this personal journey ultimately led to the development of a more philosophical approach to food. Ultimately this has given Mark a unique perspective on the hospitality sector as a whole and a healthy overview of global food culture. Mark works in Macau, China SAR at the Institute for Tourism Studies as an Invited Assistant Professor.

**Nicholas Grigoriou**

Nicholas Grigoriou has over 20 years of academic and practical marketing and international marketing experience in the banking, furniture, petroleum and education industries. Prior to entering academia, Nicholas held sales and marketing roles in the banking, furniture, and petroleum refining industries. In February 2012, Nicholas joined the Department of Marketing at Monash University's Malaysia campus, where he teaches units in marketing planning and implementation, and marketing in an international context. Nicholas was awarded a doctorate degree in philosophy from Swinburne University in 2013. His Ph.D. research investigated how packaged food and beverage exporters make product customisation and standardisation decisions for export to China. His research interests are in new product development and branding and he serves on the editorial review board of the International Journal of Business in Emerging Markets.

**Bruno Mascitelli**

Bruno is an Associate Professor at Swinburne University of Technology. He was previously employed by the Australian Trade Commission (Austrade) for 18 years based in Europe and later with the US Foreign Commercial Service based in Melbourne. Since joining academia he has taught in areas such as International Business, Australian trade and European Union matters. His publications cover numerous journal articles and book chapters as well as 11 books on themes such as organic food, international business and Australian trade and Investment.

**Grant O'Bree**

Following a career within the tourism and management industry spanning over 20 years within the Asia-Pacific and Middle Eastern regions Grant turned his hand to higher education. Since becoming a lecturer, Grant has educated a diverse background of students in Human Resource Management, Digital Marketing, Organisational Behaviour and Hospitality, Tourism and Events subjects. This also includes a role at the University of Queensland as course coordinator instructing Master of Hotel Management students in International Hotel Strategic Planning and tutoring Event Management in one of the Bachelor degree programs. As such, with an extensive range of international experiences within both academia and industry, Grant is well placed to deliver courses utilizing a holistic and well-rounded perspective. Grant currently works at the Institute for Tourism Studies, Macao SAR where he lectures in various hotel and management core subjects.

**Barry O'Mahony**

Barry O'Mahony is Professor of Services Management and Chair of the Department of Marketing, Tourism and Social Impact at Swinburne University of Technology. Barry has taught undergraduate, postgraduate and doctoral courses in Australia, Ireland, Hong Kong, Malaysia and the United States and has developed and delivered undergraduate and postgraduate programs in hospitality, events and food and beverage management. Barry is a member of the academic boards of *Le Cordon Bleu* and William Angliss Institute. He has held leadership positions within the hospitality industry internationally and has conducted numerous industry research projects. He has published in leading international journals and received best paper awards at international conferences.

**John Paull**

John Paull is a social scientist and is the editor-in-chief of the open-access peer-reviewed *Journal of Organics*. He has recently been a visiting academic at the University of Oxford. He has degrees in mathematics, psychology and environmental management. He has extensive experience in academic research, corporate research and management, training, and education. He has presented his research at international conferences including Biofach, ISOFAR, and the World Organic Congress. He has published extensively in international journals with some of his papers available at http://orgprints.org. He is the author of books including *The Value of Eco-labelling* (2009) and book chapters in *Marketing of Organic Products* (2008), *Island Futures* (2011), *Diversifying Food and Diets* (2013), and *Organics in the Global Food Chain* (2013). He is currently at the School of Land and Food, University of Tasmania, and welcomes contact at j.paull@utas.edu.au.

**Rita Parker**

Rita Parker is a Visiting Fellow, University of New South Wales at the Australian Defence Force Academy, Canberra, and a Distinguished Fellow at the Center for Infrastructure Protection, George Mason University, Virginia, USA. Her research focus is on resilience and non-traditional challenges to security and her work has been published in Australia, Malaysia, Singapore and the United States. Rita is a Board member of the Australasian Security Professionals Registry and an invited member of the US Department of Homeland Security Infrastructure Higher Education Initiative Speakers Bureau. She is a former senior policy advisor to Australian Federal and State governments with a well-established background in international security and resilience issues across a range of areas. Rita has a BA,MBA and PhD.

### Benedict Sheehy

Benedict Sheehy is an Associate Professor of Law at the Graduate School of Business & Law, at RMIT University, Australia. Benedict's research focus at the moment includes corporate control, corporate social responsibility, international law, public-private partnerships, and jurisprudence. Benedict's particular interest is in the workings of the corporation and corporate regulation with consideration given to externalities, and democratic issues. This work involves jurisprudential issues, economics, public goods and public policy.

### Jo En Yap

Jo En Yap is a Lecturer in Marketing at the Department of Marketing, Tourism and Social impact, at Swinburne University, Australia. Jo En's research focus at the moment includes consumer privacy, consumer health and well-being, consumer education, food consumption and waste, and food systems regulation. Jo En is particularly interested in examining social issues from the viewpoint of the consumer so as to inject their voices into important debates and promote consumer engagement and empowerment.

# 1

# China-Australia: Knowledge exchange to overcome future food challenges

**Bruno Mascitelli and Barry O'Mahony**

## Introduction

"To say that food is a vital part of the chemical process of life is to state the obvious, but …" (Chang 1977: 3) food and its availability has become a major societal priority along with mounting global concern about food safety, security and availability. Like access to water and energy, it is now a commodity where guarantees of quality can no longer be taken for granted which has prompted political, academic and industry focus on all elements of the human food chain. At the same time Australia and China have become economically closer to the extent that China has become Australia's largest trading partner. Food is one significant area where further expansion of this economic relationship is foreshadowed because of the complementary food related opportunities that arise between the two countries. On the one hand Australia has large tracts of potentially arable land, much of which is undeveloped. On the other, China has a large population of consumers seeking an ongoing supply of fresh, quality food. In a recent joint activity, the two governments (Australia and China) succinctly summarised each other's strengths and weaknesses which highlights their need for collaboration and partnership. The joint statement signed in December 2012 aptly noted:

> Continuing population growth and limited land and water resources, particularly in the Asia–Pacific region, have made food security a priority for many governments. As the economies in our region grow, and per capita incomes rise, consumers will increasingly demand safe, high-quality, high-protein food. Australia has earned a global reputation for its expertise in agriculture and the high quality of its produce. It still has large tracts of unused or under-utilized areas in its northern regions. Some of this land could, with investment in new productive capacity and the appropriate application of technologies, produce more food for sale on world markets. China has its own expertise in agriculture as well as a surplus of investible capital, and has developed great plans for the further development of modern agriculture. After decades of progress and growth, China has developed advanced agricultural technology in areas such as crop breeding; plant disease and insect pest prevention and control technologies; and animal disease prevention and control. Firms also spread these leading technologies internationally, and so make an important contribution to improving food production and enhancing global food security (DFAT 2012a).

Thus both nations are eager to collaborate in order to develop a more resilient food supply ostensibly for the Chinese marketplace. For this reason it could be argued that China's economic emergence on the world stage in the post 2000 years was even more important for Australia than was Japan's post war reconstruction which had a dramatic and positive effect on Australia in the 1950s and 60s. Like China, Japan in the post-war recovery period, was hungry for

Australian resources particularly coal and iron ore, however, Japan's economic slowdown saw it replaced by China in 2009. Notably the other resource consumer was South Korea which meant that Australia's three top export destinations were all in North Asia. During this time strong trade routes were developed and trade with Asia has also traversed across more than just mining and iron ore. For example, Chinese students have accessed Australian education in their hundreds of thousands becoming the number one country of origin for international students in Australia. More recently, tourism from China to Australia has grown exponentially and China is now the largest inbound tourism market to this country (Mascitelli and O'Mahony 2014).

China is now considered to be a rising economic powerhouse and, along with a number of its near neighbours, has entered what has been dubbed 'the Asian Century' (Mascitelli and O'Mahony 2014). These nations have experienced dramatic economic growth and are developing an affluent urban middle class which, amongst other things, is attracted to the purchase and consumption of Australian food and wine. As a result, although Australia is considered a relatively small food producer in global terms, the potential of the sector as a future driver of the Australian economy, based on the quality of agricultural commodities and food exports, has been recognised by all Australian political parties.

A major strength is that Australia, as a food brand, carries a strong, clean image, while china has suffered some major breaches in food standards that have undermined confidence in the local food supply. As a result, there are valuable lessons to be learned from both academic and industry perspectives to strengthen food supply chains and gain deeper insights into current and future market drivers. It is important, for example that, as producers in China adapt to regulatory change and rebuild confidence in the local food supply, Australian food exporters understand local level dynamics such as the impact of price, promotion and brand salience within the Chinese market.

## Australia: A food bowl for China?

It has become commonplace for Australia to present itself globally and to the near region of Asia as the 'food bowl of Asia'. This is both an aspiration within Australia but also recognition that the Australian food and wine industry could be big winners within the Asian century. For example, demand for food in Asia was predicted to double between 2007 and 2050, with China accounting for 43 per cent of increased demand, particularly for beef, wheat and dairy products. As evidenced in the Government's White Paper: 'Australia in the Asian Century', the food industry is strongly endorsed as a sector of engagement in the Asian region and especially in China. Australia's national objectives include being a globally competitive and productive player and, in the food context, for Australia to "enhance private and public engagement in the region and build better relationships between governments, industry and the community" (DFAT 2012b).

Food production, food supply, food logistics and food safety will become an important narrative in the joint future of Australia and the Asian region. It will equally occupy a part of the possible Free Trade Agreement with China and other Asian nations and this is already evident with the recently concluded agreements with Japan and South Korea. Trends indicate that it is a realistic ambition for Australia to become a supplier of safe, high quality food to China and to its burgeoning middle class. Within this context, the demand for Australian goods and services as well as Australian food products will increase. Australia has acknowledged this opportunity through the major White Paper 'Australia in the Asian century'. While this document is no longer necessarily representative of the current Abbott government approach, it nonetheless still makes the point that Australia will reap the benefits of this emerging middle class, particularly in the provision of health, aged care, education, household goods, tourism, banking and financial services, as well as high quality food products. The emphasis on high quality food is already showing signs of strong demand within the region and this is especially true in terms of the demand for products that are certified organic (Monk et al. 2012).

At the same time, some have cautioned that there is a level of haughtiness in Australia's claims to being the food bowl of Asia based on its "overblown rhetoric" (Maher 2014). As one media outlet noted:

> Australia did not need grandiose claims about its capability for a comprehensive trade deal with China to be hugely beneficial. 'The real opportunity comes from changing diets of China's wealthy consumers, who are willing to pay higher prices for imported food particularly if it carries certification from a country with food safety standards like Australia (Maher 2014: 23).

With this in mind it is worth noting that Australia's $50 billion-a-year food export sector risks missing out on export opportunities from the Asian-led dining boom because of regulatory burdens and the absence of key free-trade agreements. In its submission to the federal review of agribusiness policy, the peak industry body the Australian Food and Grocery Council (AFGC) urges sweeping measures, including a coordinated marketing push under a new brand of 'Trust Australia'. "The significant global opportunities for the Australian agrifood sector are in stark contrast to the challenges faced" (Boreham 2014), states the council's submission to the agricultural competitiveness taskforce. The AFGC highlights how Australia's share of global food exports to its key markets slipped from 11 per cent in 2006 to 6.5 per cent last year. This mirrors Australia's overall decline in the World Economic Forum's ranking of global competitiveness, from 16th to 21st (Boreham 2014).

## Food security, food safety and food availability: What answer?

Recent food security scares in China have highlighted the potential value of China and Australia sharing their common understanding and practices to develop a secure food industry. Although relatively small, Australia is an advanced player in the food industry and a major contributor to food industry innovation including matters related to food security and food sovereignty.

Food safety issues have undermined quality food production and consumption in China especially in areas connected to dairy products, meat and baby food. Food scandals such as the Sa Lu case as well as China's largest meat processor Shuanghui have highlighted the fragility of the security measures for Chinese safe food. These scandals led Chinese consumers to express concern with their own food industry and in some cases boycott domestic production of certain food types due to the loss of trust. In some cases, like dairy products, well-off consumers turned to imported alternatives. Thus concerns about trust in the food supply chain following these food safety scandals; coupled with the rising purchasing power of Chinese consumers has been a key factor in the growth of the quality food sector in China. Challenges within the Chinese market include perceptions of freshness, transportation and shelf life as well as some price sensitivity. The market presents major opportunities for both local and international businesses but consumer trust and brand awareness are significant issues that need to be overcome to ensure that the benefits of these opportunities accrue to those that seek to access this marketplace.

## Australian food strengths

One of Australia's key strengths is its large arable land mass populated by just over 22 million people. This is a mere 0.5 per cent of Asia's population of 4.2 billion. At the same time Australia boasts a highly developed Agricultural sector that provides a surplus of food year on year, which Sheehy (2012) asserts renders Australia capable of feeding 40 million people daily. Sheehy believes that Australian farmers are the best in the world because they operate in and have overcome an extremely harsh environment. As one of the least subsidised agricultural sectors in the world, they are responsive to the introduction of new innovations and have introduced world's best practice in every commodity produced. There is also room for further growth in production either through increased productivity or through the opening up of new land to farming.

State and Federal Government regulation is another key strength for Australia. For example, food safety legislation provides a level of confidence within the food supply chain and prescribes how food related businesses must respond to food safety incidents. This includes rapid product recalls, which provide a further strategic advantage to Australia's food brand and provides assurance for consumers (Loader & Hobbs 1999). This is particularly important in the food manufacturing sector because, according to Mike Keogh (2012). Executive Director of the Australia Farm Institute, there is a major and growing demand for sophisticated food products in the Asian region. The Australian food manufacturing sector, which represents approximately 26 per cent of total manufacturing in Australia, has the potential to deliver the sophisticated food products that the emerging middle class in Asia seeks. However, it is worth noting that while food manufacturing is a growing sector, Australia would need to double current production to increase its supply of food to Asia to one per cent of Asia's needs. It is also important to consider competition from other sources such as the United States. As a result, bilateral agreements are critical to Australia's success along with continual investment in new technology and an emphasis on increasing productivity.

## The genesis of this book?

In 2013 under the auspices of the Commonwealth Government through the Australia China Council of the Department of Foreign Affairs and Trade, Swinburne University of Technology collaborated with Chinese partner Huazhong Agricultural University, based in Wuhan to organise a workshop and seminar bringing together 20 speakers across both countries and across many segments of the food sector. Over two days and under the title of 'Knowledge Exchange of Quality Food Production and Distribution: China and Australia' themes such as agribusiness, consumer preferences, supply chain, food security and safety and food regulations were discussed and debated from both a Chinese and an Australian perspective. This project sought to harness the knowledge and expertise within Australia's food chain for a constructive knowledge exchange with China and its industry experts, regulators and academics in the food industry. The objective was to draw on existing partnerships to provide an opportunity for experts from both countries to acquaint themselves with current developments and contemporary challenges in the food sector. Both nations have challenges specific to their national circumstances which require discussion and debate. The 'think tank' and network meeting also hosted at this time sought to play a leading role in strengthening and enhancing current relationships within the region by increasing co-operation and research after the event. The expected short term outcomes include the documentation of opportunities for Australia-China collaboration as well as an understanding of where synergy can be applied across areas of food production and regulation in the future. A long term legacy will be an appreciation of the key issues and challenges that need to be addressed to improve business and government relationships between China and Australia. This will form the basis of a strategic plan developed to address key challenges in partnership with industry, government and university specialists in the future. As a result of this workshop a number of colleagues have reproduced their contributions in peer reviewed format for the purposes of this book. This permanent record therefore has the potential to foster and enhance relationships between government agencies, industry, institution's and scholars within the region, by capturing some perspectives that were presented in Wuhan in 2013.

## What is in the book?

In Chapter Two Mark Gibson and Grant O'Bree, outline the current age of food security volatility describing how, over the last three decades, a series of factors have conspired to create a global food crisis in 2007. Within this context they explore the state of food security from the perspectives of China and Australia. Their work presents statistics relating to food production in both countries highlighting the disparity between China's massive output of over 1.7 billion tonnes and Australia's at only 99 million tonnes. Despite these discrepancies however, China is a net importer of food while Australia exports approximately 60 per cent of its output. Gibson and O'Bree also note that China has also endured major food shortages in the past and as a result, there is an awareness of the importance of food security within that country. For this reason China has engaged in many strategies to alleviate the food security risk, including the purchase and lease of land in other countries. In China, however, farming in China employs over 300 million people in the production of food. Thus, agriculture and food production in China is a major contributor to economic and employment growth placing it at the forefront of that nation's priorities for some time to come.

Food shortages are not an issue in Australia, however, Australian farmers have overcome major challenges to produce high yields in areas of the country that are frequently affected by drought, floods and other climate related phenomena. The agricultural developments, research and technology that has been brought to bear in this environment are considered to be world leading. As a result, engagement between both countries in research and development, food technology, food processing, packaging and transportation across all elements of the human food cycle can be beneficial for both countries.

In Chapter Three, John Paull provides a history of organic farming and identifies opportunities and challenges for both China and Australia. He describes the Genesis of "organic farming" from 1940 when the term was first coined by Lord Northbourne in his book entitled: *Look to the Land.* He notes that Australia and China are global organic leaders. Indeed, Australia currently has the highest land mass dedicated to organic farming anywhere in the world, while China also has a strong focus on organic cultivation such that combined both countries account for 37 per cent of the global total of certified organic agricultural hectares. One reason for China's emphasis on organic, Paull explains, was to develop pollution free food which was a top priority of the then General Secretary of the Communist Party, Jiang Zemin.

In Australia, the development of organic agriculture occurred in a series of four waves of development each of which Paull discusses in his chapter. These waves first began in the 1920s and 1930s, then again in the 1940s and 1950s, with the third wave coming in the 1960s and 1970s. The fourth, and most recent, was in response to a major emphasis on organic farming in the mid-to-late 1980s following the founding of the Association for Sustainable Agriculture and the Biological Farmers Association of Australia, which today is know as Organic Australia Limited.

Paull identifies significant opportunities for Australia and China to improve and further develop the organic sector. This includes tackling issues such as pollution and reporting standards including the capture of important data, as well as brand development, premium pricing and the advancement of agricultural skills. He concludes that price premiums, success stories and increasing consumer demand will drive growth in organic produce in the future providing great opportunities for both countries to capitalise on this demand.

In Chapter Four, Yap, Sheehy and Feaver, introduce us to what they describe as "the most fundamental of all challenges facing humanity ..." (page 81), that is, providing enough food to feed the planet now and in the future. They begin by noting a number of economic concerns while also highlighting the need to coordinate national food systems and to frame and design policy and statutory frameworks that support broad objectives across the food supply chain, particularly at the consumption end. They discuss a new theoretical approach to regulation which they believe must be designed to achieve more coherent economic, environmental and health outcomes. Noting the incoherence of tackling food regulation from the perspective of various actors and stakeholders and the outcomes that each stakeholder group may seek, they highlight that such approaches to policy and regulation often result in the advancement of individual goals rather than those that have a collective, positive impact on society. As a result, frictions can arise when the most powerful actors in these scenarios dominate and overwhelm the majority view. Yap et al. proffer a systems approach in which the food system is conceptualised as a complex set of resources, linkages and relationships as a means to developing balanced and coordinated regulations that reflect the interests of all parties. They provide examples of an integrated model comprised of three subsystems and nine food cycle phases that can be used at both a macro and local level. Such a systemic approach has the capacity to consider a range of "… regulatory techniques … to address the problems of the food system" (page 104). As a result, their work and the approach that informs it, has the capacity to provide the type of regulation that can protect consumers from some of the issues that have negatively impacted the food supply chain in China and beyond.

Nicholas Grigoriou opens his chapter by highlighting the rapid growth in gross domestic product in China over the last 30 years and the benefits to Chinese society that has resulted from this economic transformation. He notes that China is now both the largest producer and consumer of food in the world and highlights the major influences on food consumption in that country. He goes on to discuss how, although China's largest cities are heavily populated, 80 per cent of the population still live in rural areas. Discussing the standardisation of products presented to the Chinese market by international corporations, he cautions global entities to consider local level culture and customs when seeking to access the Chinese market. More importantly however, he identifies the move in China from a society where malnutrition was prevalent in the past to one where the rates of obesity and diet related chronic diseases have become a major challenge. As a result, he contends that that those that export food and beverage products to China "… have a moral responsibility to customise their entire marketing mix, and in particular their product strategy to provide more nutritional content" (page 124). He contends that product labelling can promote this goal.

Rita Parker sees food as a major but non-traditional challenge to security. She presents security as a complex issue influenced by a variety of variables, processes and personalities and highlights how demand for food is growing exponentially as the population rises and resources become scarce. She cites the World Food Summit's definition of food security, which is founded on three pillars: food availability, food access, and food use. Like Yap et al., she sees a need to reframe food systems, and the legislation that support them, to include major factors and actors that can have an impact on "… a nation states overall security as well as the well-being of its civil society". For example, the World Health Organisation is an important actor or stakeholder that has a specific interest in those areas that impact on population growth, health and nutrition. As a result, these issues were considered in the African famines of the 1980s where the notion of food security was reframed to include a humanitarian dimension. Lessons learned from those disasters have also highlighted a link between the security of the nation, the security of citizens and the availability of food. Parker explains, however, that it took some time before the United Nations included the eradication of extreme poverty and hunger as a major goal, which is now reflected in its millennium development plans.

With one in eight people still suffering from hunger, Parker like Grigoriou, sees this issue as a global, moral imperative requiring political and economic change. This is particularly poignant when one considers the increase in the range and quality of food available in developed countries. Increases in protein levels per person have been significant in these countries, while there has been little improvement in Africa and parts of South East Asia. Parker cautions that although security has traditionally focused on defence against military threats, the absence of war does not necessarily mean that we live in a globally secure society. She reminds us that food has often been used as a weapon of war and it is also worth noting that food scarcity has led to revolution, rebellion and war in the not too distant past. As a result, she concludes that "food trade and economic implications are significant to the security and well-being of the nation state …", and that producing sufficient food to meet the requirements of citizens is a major goal for most countries. Thus, with China and Australia facing different food related challenges these countries have much to gain by working together.

John Dalrymple, introduces us to the food processing sector highlighting how this sector in Victoria, Australia is dominated by small and medium-sized enterprises (SMEs) and is a major employer in most developed nations. As a result, he contends that the food processing industry can play a significant role in developing, supporting and revitalising rural economies. He charts the progress of technology that has allowed local level producers to access global markets noting that when combined with "… the power of large supermarket chains and the streamlining of transportation through containerisation and container refrigeration …" access and competitiveness have improved for many food SMEs. Within this scenario local level food businesses have also been able to take advantage of co-operative networks and business clusters to improve performance and increase access to global markets. He highlights the role of migrants in Melbourne's food processing industry and highlights the gains that have been made within clusters in the northern region of Melbourne. This case study has the capacity to act as a template for future development in China, especially in the context of the development of new cities and regions within the Chinese landscape.

For example, the food processing industry in Melbourne's North began as a disparate set of businesses predominantly represented by cuisines emanating from the major countries of origin of the migrants that came to Australia in the last century. Most businesses began as small, family run, businesses but soon grew to larger entities creating significant economic and employment opportunities for production workers and support services. He charts the modernisation of the food processing industry in this region, which has included third party certification such as ISO 9000 and Hazard Analysis and Critical Control Points (HACCP) control systems to assure food safety. These food clusters have had a remarkable impact at the local level underpinning the economic wellbeing of the region and creating a product point of difference based on ethnic and fusion cuisines. Dalrymple sees an opportunity for China to develop similar urban, specialised manufacturing centres to enrich the local economy, grow local enterprises and improve the overall food supply.

## Conclusion

The quest for food has in some respects travelled 360 degrees in the last few hundred years of human civilisation. By this we mean that, in the past, human progress in developed countries was, through industrial processing and mass production, able to practically guarantee the food supply. While this of course was not the case for all nations, it was indicative of the potential of the mass production of food where basic inputs were optimised by advancing technology and supply chain innovation. However, 21st century events have refocused our attention on the fragile nature of the food supply and there is now an acknowledged need to co-operate in bringing together ideas and knowledge across the human food chain to confront emerging issues, improve food security and manage the food supply. This book shows how one small initiative has provided a platform for two countries to seek to address these problems and presents a framework for continual engagement and the further sharing of knowledge. The themes which have been explored in this book exemplify how knowledge sharing can tackle these important societal issues among partners that have complementary goals. We feel that a start has been made to address what is becoming a significant global issue within the context of China and Australia. We only hope that this discourse can be continued and extended beyond these two nations perhaps through the development of communities of practice, locally, nationally and globally.

## References


Boreham T., 2014, Call for FTAs to get food moving, *The Australian*, 5 May 2014. http://www.businessspectator.com.au/article/2014/5/5/agribusiness/call-ftas-get-food-moving, accessed 9 June 2014.

Chang, K. C. 1977, in *Food in Chinese Culture: Anthropological and Historical Perspectives*, ed. K. C. Chang, Yale University Press, New York.

DFAT 2012a, *Feeding the Future – A Joint Australia–China Report on Strengthening Investment and Technological Cooperation in Agriculture to Enhance Food Security*, Australia–China Joint Working Group, December 2012, http://www.dfat.gov.au/publications-/feeding-the-future/feeding-the-future.html#oppschinese, accessed 15 July 2014.

DFAT 2012b, Australia in the Asian century, Australian Government, Canberra, http://www.asiaeducation.edu.au/verve/_resources/australia-in-the-asian-century-white-paper.pdf, accessed 12 September 2014.

Keogh, M. 2012, 'Editorial', *Farm Policy Journal*, 9(4): iv-v.

Loader, R and Hobbs, J. 1999, Strategic responses to food safety legislation, *Food Policy* 24, 685–706.

Maher S., 2014, 'Food bowl for Asia' tag harmful, *The Australian*, 23 May 2014, Newslimited, Sydney.

Mascitelli, B and O'Mahony B. 2014, 'Australia in The Asian Century – A Critique Of The White Paper', *Australasian Journal of Regional Studies.*

Monk A., Mascitelli B., Lobo A, Bez M & Chen J, 2012, *The Australian Organic Market Report 2012*, Biological Farmers Association, Queensland.

Sheehy, M. 2012, *Australian agriculture in the Asian Century, Food Bowl or Global Farmer*, http://c.ymcdn.com/sites/www.agriculture.org.au/resource/collection/23F8EEB7-BB75-45CB-A33C-A474CDDCA1B4/Asian_Food_Bowl_Oct_19.pdf , accessed 30 September 2014.

# 2

# A Commentary on global food and nutrition security – Comparatives with China and Australia

**Mark Gibson and Grant O'Bree**

After three decades of relatively cheap and abundant food it comes as something of a shock and a wakeup call that we have seemingly entered a new era of food security volatility. Without doubt the pivotal turning point here has been the global food crisis of 2007- 2008 characterised by tight supplies and soaring food prices (Headey and Fan 2010). As the crisis unfolded the shock to the international food system reached a watershed in 2009 at which time over one billion people came to suffer the worst effects of hunger and malnutrition (WFP 2009). The political fallout was also swift and decisive. Precipitated by a cornucopia of factors including rising energy prices, diversion of food to fuel (leading to financial speculation), concomitant depreciation of the US dollar, export gameplay, natural disasters and a poorly timed global financial crisis among others, the food crisis eventually led to high level multilateral meetings which aimed to head off social and political turbulence. But as history has shown us it was too little too late. Instead ensuing food riots and escalating social unrest further exacerbated food price instability leading many experts to conclude that we have consequently entered a period of persistent volatile food prices and hence food security volatility (Sharma and Gulati 2012). Not surprisingly over recent years this has once again brought the subject of food security to the forefront of both domestic and international politics. As a result securing adequate food has now become the cornerstone of agricultural and trade policies of many countries.

Both China and Australia face the same challenges of food security and each tackles it from their own ideological, political and economic standpoints idiosyncratic in their own way. However, these challenges are not unique to these countries. Food security is a global phenomenon that daily affects every man, woman and child on the planet. Collectively we are 'in this together' which ultimately means that global food security can only really be achieved when each and every country, sovereign nation or political entity secures adequate food security on an ongoing basis for all their peoples. This is a tremendous challenge for all and like Australia and China each country aims to perfect its own preferred option or 'best practice'. Yet the challenges are numerous and again not surprisingly, the difficulties begin at the conceptual level. Understanding the many dimensions of food security, the many variables involved, as well as the co-interaction, the co-integration or the codependence of these is paramount if food security is to be achieved at both the micro and the macro levels. This is not just theoretical posturing either for when it comes to food security alone there is a vast array of definitions that, rather than aid in conceptualising the issues are seemingly open to misinterpretation, misunderstanding and selective interpretation. In fact with over 200 definitions and 450 indicators of the 'food security concept' there is sufficient confusion and complication to suit even the most discerning of tastes (Riely and Mock 1995; Gibson 2012).

Yet despite food security's intricacies and its sometimes bloated conceptual platform, simply stripping out all extraneous words, all nuances, hints and implications it can be seen that the underlying fundamental premise of the whole notion of food security is that it can only really exist when and if a person has sufficient food on an on-going basis to meet his or her requirements for an active and healthy life (Gibson 2012).

This simple proposition is best envisaged in perhaps one of the most often quoted definitions of food security – that of the Food and Agricultural Organization of the United Nations (FAO) when it suggests:

> Food security exists when all people, at all times, have physical, social and economic access to sufficient, safe and nutritious food which meets their dietary needs and food preferences for an active and healthy life (FAO 2014).

In this the FAO give rise to a concept of food security resting on a foundation of four pillars: availability, access, stability and biological utilisation. All pillars can be thought of in terms of the individual, family or country levels.

Availability is particular concerned with the supply of food – that which is either produced domestically, originating from imported sources, or both (Copeland, Frankenberger et al. 2002). Importantly, in the FAO definition this pillar also requires that the concept takes into account not only the volume or quantity of goods but also the quality of food items too (IAAH 2008). Moreover, availability is justly concerned with the 'access' dimension of infrastructure and ensuring that food reaches, or is 'available', in the markets and areas needed. Furthermore, access, more specifically – assuming adequate availability, is the notion that an individual has sufficient physical and economic resources or control at least, in his or her ability to acquire the necessary foods he or she requires (ibid). Building on these two concepts, biological utilisation refers to an individual's capacity to maximise the nutritional benefit from the foods an individual consumes. Although poorly understood for a long time, the idea that food was somehow related to good health has surely and steadily become entrenched in the whole package of food security over the ensuing decades. Thus following on from this, effective utilisation of foods then is itself is now rightly founded upon the health and vitality not only of the consumer but of the storage and preparation practices surrounding food production and preparation itself. This not only taps into things such as fresh, clean running water and things like access to primary healthcare but also ensuring sufficient technology and services all along the food chain (Gerster-Bentaya and Maunder 2008). By extension common sense tells us that stability – the remaining pillar of food security, can only really be achieved amidst the continuing stability of supplies, of access and of utilisation. This in turn rests on the economic and political stability of regions; of trade agreements; of global parity and of course on the well-being of the physical environment, not to mention the absence of natural or man-made disasters.

A lot to consider no doubt yet there is another over-riding difficulty with food security analysis – and this is as much a problem for China and Australia as it is for the rest of the world – and that is the fact that there is no direct way of measuring it. There is no direct way of determining whether a person, an individual or a country has achieved or indeed lost it. Instead, policy makers, statisticians and humanitarian groups among a host of interested parties rely on measures of proxy. The difficulty here can be seen in the fact that as early as 1995 Riely and Mock recorded over 450 individual metrics associated with the concept of food security (Riely and Mock 1995). Moreover compounding this smorgasbord of choice there was for a long time little agreement as to the best and most reliable of such metrics. That was true however until about 2001 when the Committee on Food Security (CFS) after consultation and collaboration with the Food Insecurity and Vulnerability Information and Mapping Systems (FIVIMS); the Key Indicators Database System (KIDS); and the Inter-Agency Working Group (IAWG) among others endorsed a suite of seven core indicators (Table 2.1). A further group of indicators monitoring the underlying food economy as best representing the overarching problem was also chosen to compliment the core indicators. Once again though not everyone signs up to this suite of indicators as being representative although that said, in reality it does reflect a good measure of professional consensus.

## Table 2.1 – Suite of core food security indicators

**Core Food Security Indicators**

| Core Food Security Indicators |
|---|
| Average per person dietary energy supply (DES) |
| Cereals, roots and tubers as % of DES |
| Percentage of population undernourished |
| Life expectancy at birth |
| Under 5 mortality rate |
| Proportion of children under 5 that are underweight |
| Percentage of adults with body mass index (BMI) <18.5 |

Proposed Indicators for Monitoring Underlying Conditions

| | |
|---|---|
| Economic conditions | GNP per capita<br>Growth rate in GNP per capita<br>GNP per capita at 'Purchasing Power Parity' |
| Risks, hazards, shocks | Number of countries facing food emergencies |
| Food availability | Volume of production, food use, trade, and stock changes for major food commodities, by group and by country.<br>Ratio of the 5 major grain exporters 'Supplies to Requirements'<br>Food production index |
| Food access | Gini-index of income distribution<br>People living below national poverty line<br>People living on less than $1 per day |
| Stability of availability, access and supplies | Changes in cereal production in LIFDCS with/without China & India<br>Export price movements for wheat, maize and rice<br>Variability of food prices<br>Index of variability of food production |

Source: Indicators from the Assessment of the World Food Security Situation. FAO Committee on Food Security, Twenty-seventh Session, (Rome, Food and Agriculture Organisation, 2001), (CFS 2001).

As well as the individual metrics aiming to identify the food insecure there are also composite indices; those barometers of aggregated statistics that aim to quantify food security in single ordinal range – ie food 'secure' to 'insecure' or numerically as in '1 (being food secure)' and '5 (being food insecure)' etc. However, while a welcome addition to the arsenal of data, such metrics are at best only able to gauge overall perceptions or trends rather than actual realities on the ground. Once again the challenge of finding a suitable composite index lays in the weight given to the various component metrics and any aggregates or algorithms involved, as well as to the overall adoption of one particular index over another by the many and varied stakeholders involved.

So what propels food security beyond the obvious necessity to fulfill the needs of individuals and nations? Food security is the product of a long and admiral social goal that perhaps had its zenith in the early 1970's. In fact there have been numerous calls to arms since that period but perhaps the two most notable were the United Nations World Food Conference and the Millennium Development Goals.

## United Nations world food conference

The United Nations World Food Conference (WFC) was held in Rome under the auspices of the FAO in 1974. After examining global food problems concerning production and consumption, the conference adopted a Universal Declaration outlining the target of Eradication of Hunger and Malnutrition declaring:

> Time is short. Urgent and sustained action is vital. The Conference, therefore, calls upon all peoples expressing their will as individuals, and through their Governments and non-

> governmental organisations, to work together to bring about the end of the age-old scourge of hunger (Article 12, UN 1975).

At the same conference, it was also firmly established that:

> Every man, woman and child has the inalienable right to be free from hunger and malnutrition in order to develop fully and maintain their physical and mental faculties (Article 1, UN 1975).

Importantly one affirmation that emerged from the conference was the acknowledgement that the causes of famine and food insecurity were not so much failures in food production but rather structural problems relating to poverty, inequality and other social deprivations – this was a conceptual leap and one enthusiastically adopted.

## Millennium development goals

The second noteworthy social target of food security politics over the last few decades was the Millennium Development Goals (MDG's). The MDG's were the result of the United Nations Millennium Declaration of September 8, 2000. Collectively this amounted to a list of goals (eight in total), encompassing 21 targets gathered from 62 indicators for 189 countries. Originally the aim was to work together in achieving these goals by the end of 2015 (UN 2000; UN 2000), although since then certain realities have brought some of these targets into doubt. That said the international community is still strongly aligned and fully committed in their underlying principles (UN 2005; UN 2005).

Using this quick introduction as a backdrop it is worth exploring the state of food security from both China and Australia's perspective a little more closely. For this the FAO four pillars will be used as well as the outcome or malnutrition figures. We will also look at some of the policy paradigms and other measures that place all of this data in context.

**Availability**

At the outset it is worth mentioning that is difficult to directly compare these two countries food positions as some might say it is like comparing apples with oranges. For instance on the surface according to the World Bank population data, as of 2013 Australia's population was 22.68 million while China's was 1.35 billion; that is 0.32 per cent and 19.16 per cent of total global population respectively (World Bank 2014). Furthermore figures (Table 2.2) show that according to the Food Balance Sheets[1] the latest 2009 rolling figures show that China's overall agriculture and livestock (including fish) production far outnumber that of Australia's by a good margin. In fact, topping almost 1.7 billion tonnes (number one in world output) China's output compared to Australia's total for the same year of just under 99 million tonnes highlights a huge discrepancy; a 17 fold difference. Yet this picture without explanation would be misleading.

1 FAO Food Balance Sheets; Crops Primary Equivalent = *Alcoholic Beverages, Cereals – Excluding Beer, Fruits – Excluding Wine, Miscellaneous, Oilcrops, Pulses, Spices, Starchy Roots, Stimulants, Sugar & Sweeteners, Sugarcrops, Tobacco & Rubber, Treenuts, Vegetable Oils, Vegetables.* Livestock and Fish Primary Equivalent = *Animal Fats, Aquatic Products, Eggs, Fish, Seafood, Meat, Milk – Excluding Butter, Offal.*

## Table 2.2 Total annual food production (tonnes 2009)

| | Commodity Item | Production (1000 tonnes) | | |
|---|---|---|---|---|
| | | **World** | **China** | **Australia** |
| **Total** | | 8,896,943 | 1,698,753 | 98,590 |
| **Vegetal Products** | | | | |
| | Cereals – Excluding Beer | 2,251,614 | 417,786 | 34,479 |
| | Starchy Roots | 720,407 | 156,271 | 1,221 |
| | Sugar crops | 1,890,480 | 123,430 | 30,284 |
| | Sugar & Sweeteners | 188,513 | 13,215 | 4,711 |
| | Pulses | 63,121 | 4,331 | 1,804 |
| | Treenuts | 14,316 | 2,937 | 69 |
| | Oilcrops | 489,785 | 57,824 | 2,611 |
| | Vegetable Oils | 144,162 | 18,825 | 384 |
| | Vegetables | 1,008,378 | 522,675 | 1,924 |
| | Fruits - Excluding Wine | 593,351 | 115,876 | 3,413 |
| | Stimulants | 17,307 | 1,403 | 0 |
| | Spices | 7,526 | 858 | 3 |
| | Alcoholic Beverages | 309,939 | 47,737 | 2,911 |
| **Animal Products** | | | | |
| | Meat | 284,925 | 78,089 | 3,998 |
| | Offals | 17,417 | 3,911 | 319 |
| | Animal Fats | 35,463 | 3,729 | 670 |
| | Eggs | 67983 | 27,773 | 159 |
| | Milk - Excluding Butter | 697,839 | 40,385 | 9,388 |
| | Fish, Seafood | 142,901 | 49,983 | 239 |
| | Aquatic Products, Other | 19,499 | 11,715 | 3 |
| | Miscellaneous | | | |

Source Food Balance Sheets (FAOSTAT 2014)

For one thing whilst overall production figures for Australia might be small, Australia actually currently produces nearly three times more food than it requires to feed its own population. It sells the surplus on the international market making it an overall net exporter of food. Indeed, it is estimated that at current levels, Australian food production volumes are actually sufficient to feed close to 60 million people (PMSEIC 2010). China by contrast, despite the overwhelming numbers still imports more than it exports – 106m tonnes versus 27m tonnes respectively in 2009. In fact in this respect China has been a net agricultural importer of food since 2003 (Ogilvie 2012). As a result China is very dependent on the global market for its food security and by extension carries with it all the associated risks of economic and political instability and the like.

Furthermore, while Australia has enjoyed relative abundance for a while now, China's recent history (since its creation in 1949) has been somewhat checked constantly being plagued by food shortages, famine and more than a few natural disasters. From an overarching perspective though there have been some remarkable gains, particularly in total grain output (TGO). Since its inception for instance, the People's Republic of China's (PRC) TGO has increased from 113.20 million tons to present day production values of 490 million tons while its population increased nearly 3 fold from 541.67 million to 1314.48 million in the same period. That equates to an increase from approximately 0.569 kg per capita per day in 1949 to present day values of just over 1kg per capita per day (Sharma and Gulati 2012). Whilst China has experienced remarkable agricultural output growth over this period it's most robust and sustained growth period has been since the late 1970s. More precisely between 1978-2009 China's agricultural outputs grew at about 4.4 per cent per annum. This rapid increase together and a slowdown in the growth of population combined contributing to the impressive improvement in per capita food availability. In fact during this period China's per capita calorie count increased by over 1400 kcal – quite a feat! (Sharma and Gulati 2012). Furthermore from about the mid to late 1990's China's long-term food production shortages were finally reversed. Since then agricultural production in many sectors, especially among the grain crops have gone on to produce surpluses transforming not only the agricultural landscape of China but also the value-added food production sectors.

## Changing diets

More recently too, another factor in both China and Australia's transforming crop production patterns has been in response to changing diets in which a growing affluent society is demanding more meat, vegetables and dairy produce (Zhang, Duan *et al.* 2010; Sharma and Gulati 2012). Not surprisingly, as has been the case in many similar models around the world, this has also meant better farm incomes as more money can be earned from animal husbandry and other high-added value cash crops such as fruits and vegetables etc. In China these real term increases equaled a 13.7 fold improvement between 1980 and in 2004. In Australia, on the other hand, the livestock sector (particularly in beef cattle) is a somewhat mature industry which relies on exports including those to China for sustained or increased growth. In the last few years this has been rather flat although this says more about the slower response mechanism on Australia's part than demand on China's side.

## China consumption

Production aside availability too is a product of consumption and in this respect China expresses some noteworthy figures. Currently for instance China consumes 25 per cent of the world's total soya bean production, 20 per cent of the world's corn and 16 per cent the world's wheat (Ogilvie 2012). These are staggering figures and of course the more demand there is from the Chinese community the more pressure is placed on world commodity stocks and by extension world prices – something worth considering in the overall objective of global and national food security.

### Chinese agricultural operation

So while the figures by themselves offer a mixed bag in terms of food security both within and without China's borders what the figures do hint at is the sheer scale of the Chinese agricultural operation. Due to China's huge population China's agricultural production and trade is a global powerhouse – especially when it comes to grains. This undoubtedly contributes further to the food security of other countries, yet this level of production requires much more consideration in terms of political, economic and physical infrastructures. For instance farming in China is far more pervasive than in Australia, and many other parts of the world for that matter. That is to say – China employs over 300 million people in the farming sector on approximately 9,327,489 sq km arable land (equivalent to a whopping 10 percent of all arable land worldwide) (FAOSTAT 2014). Compare this to Australia whereby agricultural land occupies a mere 5.6 per cent of total land mass in that country and the opportunities for China, according to the World Bank seem enormous (World Bank 2014). If China were to increase efficiency and productivity yields to match that of Australia for instance, China would have the potential to increase cereal production alone to over 650 million tonnes – that would equate to a mammoth 18.55 per cent of all cereal production worldwide. Compare this to Australia's 1.53 per cent and the scales are somewhat tipped.

## Fish

Another area of great disparity and one worth highlighting is in the fish and seafood sector. China has an annual fish and seafood industry topping close to 50 million tonnes dwarfing Australia's near 240 thousand tonnage. Although to be fair, in terms of sustainable food security as Chinese diets demand greater fish protein, it has to be said is that this level of demand runs great risk from potential overfishing. In this respect careful consideration must be given to the future of the industry if stock levels are to be maintained or even increased (AusAid 2011).

## Australia's agricultural operation

Compared to China, Australia's agricultural sector is miniscule although considered by many, if one were to take into account prevalence of industrialisation and mechanisation, to be more mature, more progressive and certainly more intensive. Australia's farming sector on the whole is well funded operating a healthy research and development budget with the caveat that more research is required. This has come about for many reasons mainly borne of necessity; for one thing Australia suffers vast climatic variation and desertification and must innovate solutions to these challenges. On the whole then with its enormous arable land area, technical expertise and innovation, Australia continues to produce highly sought after quality products. In fact Australian agriculture is stalwartly export orientated and a significant competitor in the global agricultural export market accounting for 12 per cent of Australia's overall GDP. Australia is a major exporter of sugar as well as being the largest exporter of goat meat and the second largest beef exporter in the world.

Lastly, due to low government subsidies and support (four per cent of farm income) farmers are among the most self-sufficient producers in the world. This helps to perpetuate transparency in the regulatory environment and instill trust when it comes to foreign investment and genuine competitiveness.

## Poverty

Access to food depends on a multitude of variables including income and distribution of income; share of expenditure on food; agriculture's contribution to GDP; and the level of employment, among other things. In this mix, personal poverty metrics are perhaps the single most important variable that is quoted when it comes to determining access to food. In this though the data is somewhat one-sided for although there is no doubt poverty in Australia the World Bank does not collect data on this 'developed' country – as poverty is considered negligible on the global platform. China by contrast is a different story with just over 11.8 per cent living on less than \$1.25[2] a day in to 2009 (World Bank 2014). That said China is making good progress in this area. In the space of 6 years it has witnessed a marked and steady decline of its rolling average poverty statistics which in fact fell from 28 per cent of the population in 2002 to less than 17.5 per cent in 2005 and 13 per cent in 2008. Although having said that if we were to raise the threshold slightly to those living on less than \$2-a-day the picture still remains a little bleak with figures still hovering at a scary 27.2 per cent of the population[3]. As mentioned, the trend remains steady and in the right direction. There have been many factors in China's success in this area. In particular concerted

---

2 Population below \$1.25 a day is the percentage of the population living on less than \$1.25 a day at 2005 international prices.

3 For the sake of fairness this figure has dropped from over 50 per cent in 2002.

and targeted policies of rural industrialization, as well as measures enhancing off-farm employment have both played important roles in bringing these figures down.

As well as increasing wealth and by extension access to food China has also embarked on widespread strategies aimed at increasing the country's overall food security through increased social policies and safety nets (Sharma and Gulati 2012).

Although poverty thresholds are often the default metric when it comes to access, other ways of assessing the level of accessibility are things like the prevalence or percentage of roads paved; technology infrastructure; and of course the number of markets available.

## Chinese manufacturing

In overall access strategies it has to be said that China currently has a more progressive outlook than it has had at any other time in its recent history. In helping this along China too is increasingly opening up its agricultural supply chain to foreign trade and investors. One area in particular in which in-roads can be made by foreign direct investment in the Chinese agricultural supply chain is through the food manufacturing and the value-added sectors. Although like so many others nowadays China too is beginning to feel the pinch of higher costs of labour and other inputs challenging the long held low-cost, high-output model of productivity. Though no doubt positive progress in the right direction it has been said that much more still needs to be done in order to reduce subsidies and support for Chinese State Owned Enterprises (SOE's) to effectively level the playing field (Ogilvie 2012).

## Australia's manufacturing

Australia's food manufacturing sector by contrast already suffers from higher input costs including raw materials and labour; although, it is also very aware of this shortcoming. To combat this disadvantage and give themselves an edge in terms of continued food security Australia realises it needs to innovate through research and development which it does well.

Another area where Australia focuses its food security approach both domestically (particularly when it comes to remote Indigenous communities) (COAG 2009) and within their external food aid programme is through access. They achieve this through a dual approach by increasing availability of food through production; by improving trade; and at the same time increasing the poor's accessibility through job creation and safety nets. In improving the social and physical infrastructures Australia has prioritised three pillars namely;

1. the lifting of agricultural productivity through increased agricultural research and development;
2. Improving rural livelihoods by strengthening market infrastructures and market access;
3. Building community resilience into the social fabric by supporting the establishment and improvement of social protection programs.

Collectively these pillars aim to increase the food available in both markets and poor households whilst increasing the incomes and employment opportunities of poorer men and women alike. In this Australia is committed with food security expenditure expecting to grow strongly over the next few years (AusAid 2011).

## Utilisation

In lieu of a direct measure of food utilisation several of the more often quoted of the metrics are the outcome measures. The outcome measures are useful tools in understanding direct effects of food insecurity. Such measures also act to assess the success, or otherwise of any targeted intervention programmes. Once again though, as with the measures of proxy choosing the right outcome metric is problematic. In this there are as many critics of such measures as there are advocates and indeed many institutions regularly use several measures to draw overall pictures. Without doubt one of the most commonly used measures is the FAO's Prevalence of Undernourishment figures (AusAid 2011; FAO 2013). These figures can be measured in one of two ways the first – favoured by the FAO, is calculated on the basis of three key parameters: average food consumption (or availability of food) per person; inequality of access; and minimum calorie requirement for the average person – this is then weighted by the population demographic (MDG 2000). The second are the anthropometric measures, often but not always of the under 5's. These figures are then extrapolated to the entire population. This is because the under 5's are considered very susceptible to malnutrition and would be among the first groups to display signs of under nutrition and therefore act as a good barometer of the total population.

Anthropometric measures of child nutritional status show that China has made remarkable progress in reducing malnutrition. This has been particularly evident in the reduction of the prevalence of undernourishment figures from 18 per cent in 1990-92 to approximately 10 per cent in 2005-07 (Sharma and Gulati 2012). However, despite this improvement over the last decade or so China is still has an undernourished population in the region of 11.4 per cent or 158 million people (Morton 2012; FAOSTAT 2014).

While there are no figures for the undernourished in Australia, figures are said to be insignificant at below 2.5 per cent according to the FAO (FAOSTAT 2014) or a total prevalence for food insecurity in the region of five per cent according to Burns (Burns 2004; Rosier 2011). While these figures might be on the low end of the scale it does serve to highlight the fact that food security is not the sole preserve of 'Third World' or 'developing' countries. Indeed despite these low figures one report suggests that Australia might not be as food secure as a superficial look at the statistics might actually suggest (Reeves, Mackenzie et al. 2011).

Another of the outcome measures is the mortality rates particularly with the under-fives. While China's mortality rates, recorded by the World Bank (2012), remains at about 14 deaths per 1,000 live births or 1.4 per cent whereas, Australia's under-five mortality rate is at 4.9 per 1,000 live births (or 0.49 per cent). Interestingly though despite these low statistics on Australia's part, reports by PMSEIC (2010) indicate that the greatest potential food security threat facing Australian's relate more to public health issues stemming from insufficient nutritional value in the consumption and use of inappropriate food groups rather than a shortage per se (PMSEIC 2010; FAOSTAT 2014). Building on this, one area that is receiving a lot of attention these days and one that is not necessarily too far removed from the food security issue is the continuum of malnutrition that covers under- to over-nutrition. Overnutrition or obesity is fast becoming major health issues not only for Australia and China but it is a trend that is being replicated the world over. In China's favour is the huge media attention the problem is receiving now although whether that is sufficient to dislodge the growing trend remains to be seen. Statistically according to OECD data (2008) however while China's prevalence of obesity (age 20+) is only 5.6 per cent compared to Australia's 25.1 per cent in actual numbers, because of the population differential this equates to just

5.5 million obese people in Australia compared to a staggering 75.6 million people in China. Having looked at the above three pillars in a little more detail it serves to highlight the very different ways in which food security is viewed, measured and thus targeted.

### Stability

Few of these metrics by themselves are reliable indicators of food security without considering the variables of stability. However, the area of stability is broad and spans many disciplines of political, economic, social and environmental.

### Food price volatility

In terms of food price volatility for instance, whilst globally we mentioned we have entered a new era of price volatility – in China's situation, due to various domestic price support policies and managed trade environments they encounter a little more stability than many (Sharma and Gulati 2012). Although even this relative stability has to be weighed against the general increased integration of global commodity and financial markets as what this means is that ultimately there are more and more calls for greater transparency, regulation and monitoring of these markets for ensuring such stability (Sharma and Gulati 2012).

### Occurrence of natural disasters

Both China and Australia have weathered their fair share of natural disasters – (see figures 2.1 and 2.2).

**Figure 2.1 – Number of disasters – global to 2013**

Source: EM-DAT 2014

Increasing occurrences of deadly floods, droughts, sandstorms, hailstorms and even fire have all colluded to tighten supplies and place upward pressure on food prices. Indeed Australia weathered several droughts in the 80s 90s and more recently from 2006 to 2010. It has also been struck by widespread floods and other extreme weather patterns with Cyclone Larry wiping out more than 80 per cent of Australia's banana crops in 2006 alone. More recently another cyclone 'Yasi', went on to devastate over $US800 million worth of crops in 2011. China too suffered in 2011 with several floods reducing vegetal crop production by 20 per cent and increasing prices by as much as 40 per cent (Ogilvie 2012).

**Figure 2.2 – Number of deaths due to natural disasters to 2013**

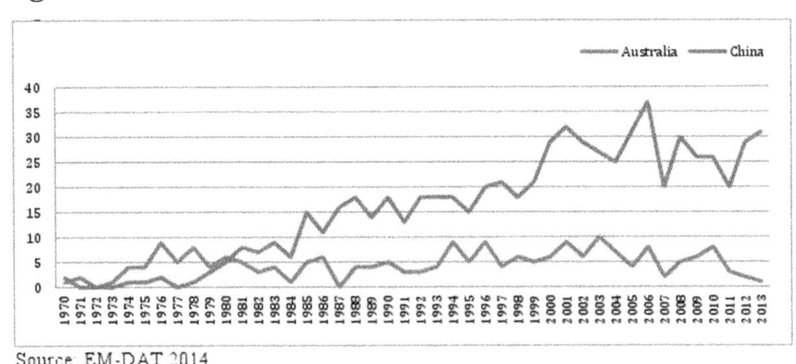


Source: EM-DAT 2014

Although, once again by way of balance in a FAO statistical data indicates that whilst there has certainly been numerous challenges in effecting stability in recent times, the overall impact has been far less than earlier predictions with only relatively moderate changes to prices for the end consumer than was previously expected (FAOSTAT 2014).

## Policy goals stability

### China's goals

So what is China's stated position on food security? Over the last few decades China has adopted aggressive agricultural expansion policies in attempts to become at least 95 per cent self-sufficient. Yet in more recent years whilst China might espouse the virtues and indeed adopt a policy of food sovereignty or self-sufficiency with regards to food security, the reality is a little different. In January 2012 the Director of the Chinese Communist Party's top policy making body for rural affairs Chen Xiwen announced that China had finally decided to stop pursuing its goal of self-sufficiency in food.

Instead, China realised that with growing population's food

demands currently being met by the substantial imports it was going to be very difficult to turn the clock back. Thus being heavily reliant on the international community China now adopts a dual food security strategy aiming to take advantage of both domestic and international resources (Hongzhou 2013; Perkowski 2013). This dual strategy looks to improve several areas from domestic production – by heavily investing in modernisation and agricultural technologies, to improving crop yields to resource efficiency drives all the while increasing overall labour productivity. All the while it is also looking at basic water and rural infrastructure as well as new improved marine and fisheries technologies in an effort to boost overall domestic production.

On the international track China's outward-looking food security policy comprises four major components:

- In the first instance in the coming years more food imports from the international market will be a necessity. Indeed by 2012 China became the world's largest importer of agricultural products;
- To help secure this stream China has been busy building new and cementing existing agricultural trade ties with the world's major food exporters, signing agreements with countries such as the United States, Canada, Thailand, Argentina and Australia;
- Secondly, concerned with the over-reliance on the international grain market China has taken measures and become one of the major players in a practice called land-grabbing – that is purchasing or leasing land in foreign countries for agricultural production. Having acquired as much as over 3.5 million hectares of land overseas China can basically boost its food supply by simply expanding its agricultural operations overseas;

- In the third dimension China is taking a more proactive albeit some say reluctant role in global food security governance. For while China is looking for security of food it is also quick to rationalize the fact that being highly dependent on the global food trade, the easiest way to safeguard its own food security is to ensure overall global food security in the first place. In this China is fast becoming a major donor in the food/humanitarian sector;
- Fourthly, and partly a follow on from the third aspect China is taking more interest in the global food market especially in areas of trade and investment. Notably China considers the deadlock of the Doha Round of trade talks as major barrier to effective global agricultural trade liberalisation. Indeed in further support of this outward looking policy Beijing has formed a working group of ministries from agriculture to commerce to facilitate and push forward such initiatives (Hongzhou 2013).

## Australia's goals

Australia has its own strengths relevant to building a food secure nation too. Perhaps the most obvious is the fact that the Australian agriculture sector maintains its leading position of producing food on the driest continent rife with low quality soils around the world. Moreover they continue to do so in the face of very harsh and continued climate variability. In this effort Australia has a strong research and development (R&D) base ranking it among the best in the world. Research and development too, not only on the agricultural sector but also of human health and nutrition. This is coupled with widespread campaigns inspiring awareness of the nutritional value of food at both the production and consumption levels around the country.

In fact on the R&D front Australia suggests that if the world is to double the food production by 2050 (as is required to meet demand) an on-going annual research and development budget equalling five per cent of 1970s gross domestic product would be required simply to ensure that the number of hungry does not increase from current levels (Reeves, Mackenzie et al. 2011).

## Aid

One side issue when it comes to both China and Australia's food security position is their participation on the world stage. This might be seen through political or economic means through governance or stewardship as well as their relative positions on Aid. In Australia's case, it has built strong links and capabilities in delivering technological development to developing countries throughout the region. In doing so, of all the OECD member countries, Australia had made the most substantial increase to their AID budget. Indeed Australia's AID strategy is to enhance developing countries internal capabilities through such platforms as markets, policy and practice in the hope of creating sustainable, autonomous and self-reliant food and agriculture production structures which in turn benefits themselves and others.

China too has ratcheted up its agricultural and food aid assistance package upwards to become a major player now helping many countries combat hunger. Furthermore China is increasingly willing to cooperate at the international level on many issues of food security.

## Discussion

This brief foray into the food security position of both China and Australia vis-à-vis the rest of the world is illuminating in the way that both countries view their food security needs and their relative strengths and weaknesses. The challenges surrounding food security are considerable and will remain so for decades to come.

Australia and China share many common interests and cooperation between the two has the potential to contribute significantly to improving food security in both regions in this period. Both are major agricultural producers at the forefront of agricultural innovation, research and development. Both have considerable experience in such challenges in dry-land agriculture as well as challenges of limited water and land resources. This together with the increasing frequency of natural disasters associated with climate change provides a rich seam of knowledge transfer potential that other countries facing similar problems can tap into. Yet despite facing a constant battle of resource and environmental constraints China has now reached critical mass in its ability for self-sufficiency in basic foods – namely cereals or grains. China is one of the world's largest producers of grains. Furthermore Beijing continues to encourage the outsourcing of agricultural production overseas through direct and indirect investments both horizontally and vertically and through uni- or multilateral agricultural development projects. To this end the Chinese Government has developed the 12th Five-Year Plan on National Agriculture and Rural Economic Development (2011–2015) to steer China's agricultural production and development policies particularly in the areas of foreign investment in agri-food businesses.

Australia too faces its own unique set of challenges and in comparison with the rest of the world it produces much less food than many other countries. But despite this Australia is still a leading supplier of beef, lamb, wheat, barley, sugar as well as dairy products to world markets and able to export well over half of its total annual agri-food production. Yet in this area, as with China, Australia needs to adapt to a changing landscape that requiring improvements in areas of infrastructure, productivity limits and essential R&D. Facilitating these needs the Australian Government's forthcoming National Food Plan stands to be a welcome blueprint for future food security development (DFAT 2012).

## Re-examining the relationship

In light of these and many other factors of food security it is evident that humanity needs to re-examine its relationship with food. Indeed if the imperatives were not clear before there certainly now exists strong economic and humanitarian obligations for reforming the international food landscape to better align itself with contemporary realities. After four decades of relative security and stability of supplies where governance in the form of the United Nations and the Americans was evident the new paradigm is being drawn. One in which emerging developing countries like India and China, have the potential to redraw the rules of engagement in terms of ideology and practice. Moreover while China has the potential to be a global leader in food security hegemonic governance Australia is the physical capacity to contribute greatly to global solutions for although Australia accounts for less than three per cent of global food trade, they are among the most efficient net food exporting nations in the world.

Indeed, global agricultural production can be summed up in a similar vein to China and Australia's examples in which one is facing severe shortage of land and water resources, while the other faces challenges of climate variability and poor soils. In such cases, as is being reflected around the increasingly globalised world is a trending deepening division of labour and specialization of commodities. In such a food landscape food self-sufficiency is not a practical and efficient approach to any country's food security position; and one in which China has come to reluctantly accept.

And while a number of countries have at times aimed for national food self-sufficiency, in many cases, a more realistic objective is food self-reliance – that is being able to earn sufficient foreign exchange from other exports so as to be able to import food. Therefore as China moves beyond food self-sufficiency, its integration into the global food system is inevitable. This brings both opportunity and challenges to global food security; one in which countries like Australia can contribute in a win-win mutually beneficial partnership (ESCAP 2009; PMSEIC 2010; Zhang, Duan et al. 2010).

## Governance

As a result of the above, it is not surprising that the question of who is responsible for the nation, the state, the world's food security is often raised. Should it be assigned to the individual; the government or state itself; or perhaps to a multilateral body or institution? Moreover, further questions are raised such as are we to work collaboratively as a global collective? Or are the self-interests of nations to be put before those of the wider community? And alas, in the wider debate do we provide solutions, or simply the means to solutions? Of course these are questions beyond the purview of this chapter but in general when it comes to governance the United Nations (UN) is seen as one choice along with the USA, various EU agencies and other small but influential think tanks and charitable organisations. All these bodies have contributed to the many and various targets addressing food security over the years; however perhaps the most notably celebrated of these are the 1974 World Food Conference (WFC) and the Millennium Development Goals (MDG).

In fact in terms of global governance China's hegemony may even surpass that of America's especially when considering recent years' efforts. In this China no doubt impacts the wider global community.

Very much an active, and albeit in Morton's (2012) words a 'reluctant' global governance stakeholder it remains to be seen in just what way China's emerging role is likely to shape the future direction of many aspects of the international food sector (Morton 2012). For China achieving food security means more than the engineering of a sustainable supply chain it ultimately means stability both politically and economically (Ogilvie 2012).

China and Australia can both contribute significantly to global food security. Yet one could almost succinctly sum up the global challenges of food security in the dichotomy that sees Australia as having the greatest per capita average of resources of any country in the world leaving China with the least (DFAT 2012). Yet even despite this disadvantage simply by virtue of its size what happens in China matters on the world stage. This is true of any shortfalls in China's production as well as any surpluses or bumper cash crops traded on the global market (ACQ 2013). Indeed China's impact on price volatility and stability are already having a marked impact on the global stage – particularly in the context of the Sino-Australian relationship.

## References

ACQ (2013). Australia's future in China's food security. *Australia China Quarterly*.

DFAT (2012). *Feeding the future: a joint Australia–China report on strengthening investment and technological cooperation in agriculture to enhance food security*. Australia–China Joint Working Group. Australia, Australia. Dept. of Foreign Affairs and Trade: 88.

AusAid (2011). *Sustainable economic development: Improving food security. Australia, Australian Aid*: 11.

Burns, C. (2004). *A review of the literature describing the link between poverty, food insecurity and obesity with specific reference to Australia*. Melbourne, Victorian Health Promotion Foundation.

CFS (2001). *Suggested core indicators for monitoring food security status*. FAO Committee on Food Security, Twenty-sixth Session, Rome, Food and Agriculture Organisation.

COAG (2009). *National strategy for food security in remote indigenous communities*. Australia, The Council of Australian Governments: 9.

Copeland, R., T. Frankenberger, et al. (2002). *Food and nutrition technical assistance project assessment*. Washington, DC, The United States Agency for International Development.

EM-DAT (2014). Emergency Events Database EM-DAT, Centre for Research on the Epidemiology of Disasters.

ESCAP (2009). *Sustainable agriculture and food security in Asia and the Pacific*, United Nations Economic and Social Commission for Asia and the Pacific (ESCAP): 123.

FAO. (2013). Food Security Indicators from http://www.fao.org/economic/ess/ess-fs/fs-data/en/#.Un2n-iebFmp, Retrieved July, 2014.

FAO (2014). Food Security Statistics, Food and Agriculture Organisation.

FAOSTAT (2014). Food and Agriculture Statistics, Food and Agriculture Organisation.

Gerster-Bentaya, M. and N. Maunder (2008). Food security concepts and frameworks: what is food security?, EC-FAO.

Gibson, M. (2012). *The feeding of nations: re-defining food security for the 21st century.* Boca Raton, Florida, CRC Press.

Headey, D. and S. Fan (2010). *Reflections on the global food crisis: how did it happen? How has it hurt? And how can we prevent a next one?* IFPRI Research Monograph 165. Washington, DC, International Food Policy Research Institute.

Hongzhou, Z. (2013). *China's food security: from self-sufficiency to a dual strategy.* RSIS COMMENTARIES No. 045/2013. Nanyang, China, S.Rajaratnam School of International Studies, NTU.

IAAH. (2008). Interview with Mr. Kostas Stamoulis, Secretary General of the Committee on World Food Security from http://www.iaahp.net/fileadmin/templates/iaah/pdf/Interview_Stamoulis.pdf, Retrieved July, 2014.

MDG. (2000). Proportion of population below minimum level of dietary energy consumption from http://mdgs.un.org/unsd/mdg/Metadata.aspx?IndicatorId=5 Retrieved 10 July 2008, 2008.

Morton, K. (2012). *Learning by Doing: China's role in the global governance of food security.* RCCPB Working Paper #30. Bloomington, Australia, Research Center for Chinese Politics & Business: 41.

Ogilvie, C. (2012). *Opportunities for China and Australia in food security.* KPMG: Cutting through comlpexity. Australia, KPMG: 32.

Perkowski, J. (2013, 12 March 2014). Feeding China's population, Forbes, from http://www.forbes.com/sites/jackperkowski/2013/04/25/feeding-chinas-population/, Retrieved August, 2014.

PMSEIC (2010). Australia and food security in a changing world. Canberra, Australia, The Prime Minister's Science, Engineering and Innovation Council.

Reeves, T., R. Mackenzie, et al. (2011). *Food security issues for the Australian horticulture industry.* Fortitude Valley QLD, HAL project AH09009: 62.

Riely, F. and N. Mock (1995). *Inventory of food security impact indicators: food security indicators and framework. A Handbook for Monitoring and Evaluation of Food Aid Programs.* Arlington, VA, IMPACT.

Rosier, K. (2011). *Food insecurity in Australia: What is it, who experiences it and how can child and family services support families experiencing it?* CAFCA Practice Sheet. Australia, CAFCA.

Sharma, P. and A. Gulati (2012). *Approaches to food security in Brazil, China, India, Malaysia, Mexico and Nigeria: lessons for developing countries.* policy series no.14. India, Indian Council for Research on International Economic Relations.

UN (1975). *Report of the World Food Conference 1974.* New York, United Nations.

UN (2000). *Millennium Summit: The UN Millennium Declaration.* The Millennium Assembly of the United Nations, New York, United nations.

UN (2000). *United Nations Millennium Declaration.* United Nations, UN. A/RES/55/2.

UN (2005). *2005 World Summit Outcome. Fact Sheet.* New York, United Nations Department of Public Information.

UN (2005). Draft resolution referred to the high-level plenary meeting of the general assembly by the general assembly at its fifty-ninth session: 2005 World Summit Outcome. United Nations, UN. A/60/L.1.

WFP. (2009). The World Food Programme: Billion for a Billion – How can the online billion help the hungry billion? from http://www.wfp.org/videos/billion-billion-how-can-online-billion-help-hungry-billion, Retrieved July, 2014.

World Bank. (2014). Website of the WorldBank from http://www.worldbank.org/, Retrieved 13th March 2014, 13th March 2014.

World Bank. (2014). Website of the WorldBank: Poverty and Equity from http://povertydata.worldbank.org/poverty/country/CHN, Retrieved 13th May 2014, 13th May 2014.

Zhang, Z., Z. Duan, et al. (2010). Food Security of China: The Past, Present and Future. *Plant Omics Journal* 3(6): 183-189.

# 3

# Opportunities and challenges for organic food and agriculture: China and Australia

John Paull

## Introduction

We cannot poison our way to prosperity. This is the foundational premise of organic agriculture. Organic food is food grown without the use of synthetic pesticides and fertilisers, without genetically modified organisms (GMOs), nanotechnology or irradiation. Such agriculture has a proven track record over millennia. An industrial process demonstrated by Fritz Haber and Carl Bosch in 1909 changed the practice of agriculture (and warfare) by producing cheap and abundant synthetic fertiliser (and explosives) (Smil 2001). The Haber-Bosch process captures nitrogen from the air, commonly referred to as 'fixing nitrogen', and ushered in an era of high external input chemical agriculture. There soon developed a call to reject the use of synthetic chemical inputs in the production of food.

The call for an agriculture that eschews chemical inputs dates from the Agriculture Course presented by Dr. Rudolf Steiner in the summer of 1924 at Koberwitz (now Kobierzyce, Poland) (Paull 2011a; Steiner 1924). Steiner called for his farming ideas to be experimentally tested, developed and refined and, after that, disseminated. This injunction culminated in the publication of Ehrenfried Pfeiffer's book *Bio-dynamic Agriculture and Gardening* (Paull 2011c; Pfeiffer 1938).

The term 'organic farming' was coined by Lord Northbourne in his book *Look to the Land* (Northbourne 1940; Paull 2006) and this coincided, according the a World Health Organisation account, with the first use of synthetic pesticides, also in 1940 (WHO 2008). Northbourne had been a lecturer in agriculture at Oxford University, he was a biodynamic farmer, and he invited and hosted Dr. Pfeiffer to present a conference on biodynamics at his estate in Kent in 1939 (Paull 2011b). Northbourne's manifesto of organic agriculture *Look to the Land* followed shortly after that biodynamics conference. His book posited a contest of two mutually exclusive food production philosophies, of 'chemical farming' versus 'organic farming'. Northbourne was under no illusions that this would be a quick victory for the organics idea: "it is a task for generations of concentrated effort, slow and laborious ... And those engaged will be fighting a rearguard action for many decades, perhaps for centuries" (Northbourne 1940: 115).

The International Federation of Organic Agriculture Movements (IFOAM) was founded in Versailles, France, in 1972 to represent the interests of the organics sector. From the outset it brought together the diversity of kindred associations including organic and biodynamic associations, and the Soil Association (Paull 2010). The proposer, Roland Chevriot, of the French organic association *Nature et Progrès*, made it clear, in his proposing letter, that diversity was welcomed, where he wrote of "this federation respecting all particularities and individualities" (Chevriot 1972). There are currently 732 IFOAM affiliated organisations from 114 countries (Willer & Lernoud 2014). National and international standards have been developed and third party certification provides assurance to consumers and facilitates the international trade in organic food.

Australia and China are both global organic leaders. When pitted against the more than 160 countries that report organic agriculture statistics, both countries regularly score in the Organics Olympiads (Paull 2011e, 2012). Australia with 12,001,724 hectares, and China with 1,900,000 hectares, together account for 37 per cent of the global total of 37,544,909 certified organic agricultural hectares (Willer & Lernoud 2014). Australia is in first position and China is in fourth position in terms of certified organic agricultural hectares from a total of 164 countries reporting organics data (with Argentina and USA in positions two and three). The top ten organics countries account for 80 per cent of global certified organic agricultural hectares. Australia and China have led the world in organics growth over the past decade (2001-2011) with decadal increments of 4,346,800 and 1,844,361 hectares respectively, and together account for 32 per cent of the global growth over the decade (Paull 2011f).

Globally there are 4.6 million tonnes of chemical pesticides delivered annually into the environment, just one per cent of these are effective while "99 per cent of pesticides applied are released to non-target soils, water bodies, and atmosphere, and finally absorbed by almost every organism" (Zhang, Jiang & Ou 2011: 133). This global dispersal of synthetic pesticides is scandalous, wasteful, and dangerous. In China there are a reported 100,000 deaths to pesticide per year (Zhang et al. 2011). The goal of organic agriculture has always been to be part of the solution rather than to be part of the problem. China and Australia have very different strengths and weaknesses and the advancement of the organics enterprise can best be progressed by playing to their different respective strengths. Some comparative data are presented in Table 3.1.

**Table 3.1: Australia and China compared**

| Parameter | Australia | China |
|---|---|---|
| Country Area | 774.1 m ha | 960.0 m ha |
| Agricultural Area | 409.7 m ha | 519.1 m ha |
| Arable Land | 47.7 m ha | 111.6 m ha |
| Forest | 148.4 m ha | 209.6 m ha |
| Population | 23,340,000 | 1,416,670,000 |
| Rural Population % | 10.5% | 46.2% |
| Total Labour Force | 12,320,000 | 850,580,000 |
| Labour Force in Agriculture | 460,000 | 502,210,000 |
| Labour Force in Agriculture % | 3.73% | 59.04% |
| Agricultural Land per person working in agriculture | 104.3 ha | 0.25 ha |
| Fertilizer Use on agricultural land | 46.3 kg/ha | 548.3 kg/ha |
| Food Imported value | US $705 m from China to Australia | US $7,775 m from Australia to China |
| Certified Organic Agriculture | 12,001,724 ha | 1,900,000 ha |
| Certified Organic Agriculture % of agricultural land | 2.93% | 0.36% |
| Certified Organic Wild Collection | 0 ha | 982,400 ha |
| Organic Retail Sales | €927.0 m | €790.8 m (but maybe >US $2b) |
| Organic Exports | €101.6 m | €235.5 m |

Sources: FAO, 2014a, 2014b; FAOSTAT, 2014a, 2014b; Willer & Lernoud, 2014; World Bank, 2014.

The majority of consumers who purchase organic food do so for health reasons. In a global survey (N=21,100), "Over two thirds of survey respondents think that organic foods are healthier for them and their children" (Nielsen 2005b: 4). A global survey across 38 countries reported that the reasons for purchasing organic are "healthier for me" (51 per cent), "healthier for my children" (17 per cent), "better for the environment" (15 per cent), "kinder to animals" (seven per cent) and "other" (10 per cent) (Nielsen 2005a).

## Organic China

China has long been presented as an example to the world of how to farm organically. While Haber and Bosch were developing their process for producing synthetic fertiliser, a US Professor of agriculture, Hiram King, was pursuing a very different path, travelling through China and carefully documenting and recording its traditional agricultural practices. In his resulting book *Farmers of Forty Centuries* he praised the practices that he witnessed. He declared that "China ... long ago struck the keynote of permanent agriculture ... it remains for us and other nations to profit by their experience" (King 1911: 274). Many editions of King's groundbreaking book have appeared in the century since it first appeared. *Farmers of Forty Centuries* is regarded as an organic agriculture classic (Paull 2011d) and the book has recently appeared in a Chinese translation (King 2011).

In the latter part the twentieth century, the traditional farming practices of China were supplanted by the so-called Green Revolution and the widespread embrace of chemical agriculture. There was a parallel increase in farm mechanization, with the power of agricultural machinery growing by a factor of 28 in the years 1970 to 2003 (Li 2005). These innovations produced a surge in food production, but close on the heels of this were the dysfunctional manifestations of the Green Revolution. Even in a totalitarian state, accounts of "poisoned food" (Zong 2002: 55), the deaths of farmers from pesticides (Giovannucci 2005), and the deaths of consumers from poisoned produce (McKinna 2006) are news that is beyond suppression. Events such as the exclusion of Chinese produce from the Japanese market because of pesticide residues (Latner & Lei 2006) and the melamine-in-baby-formula scandal in which at least six children died, 300,000 were sick, several senior managers were executed, and others imprisoned for life (Associated Press 2009), have been wake-up calls for China.

The then Communist Party General Secretary, Jiang Zemin, had urged a "vigorous adjustment of agricultural structure" and, as a "top priority ... establish quality standards for farm produce, and move to a system for examining and testing farm produce and to develop organic and pollution-free food" (*People's Daily* 2001).

China was been a late-comer to the international organics movement. Organics in China dates from 1990, with the first certified organic export from China being tea exported to the Netherlands and certified by the Dutch certifier, SKAL (Zong 2002). In 1990 the Ministry of Agriculture (MoA) created the Green Food programme, and in 1992 set up the China Green Food Development Centre (CGFDC). Following a separate path, the State Environment Protection Administration (SEPA) set up the Organic Food Development Centre (OFDC) in 1994 (Paull 2007). The philosophies behind these two moves were different. Green Food is a local certification scheme focused on certifying the process of production and testing the product for reduced pesticide residues. SEPA with its organic programme had an eye on gaining a premium for exports and encouraging more sustainable on-farm practices.

The CGFDC certified to two standards, Green Food Grade A and Green Food Grade AA, and the latter was incrementally converged with international organic standards. One advantage of this scheme is that there is a pathway to organic certification which recognizes the intermediate achievement of Green Food Grade A, and there is thereby a defined pool of potential candidates for conversion to organic.

The Certification and Accreditation Administration of China (CAAC) in 2005 issued the first national organic standards for China, the Chinese National Standards for Organic Produce. Since 2005 there has been a single organic logo for China, which is a bilingual logo, Chinese and English, and comes in two versions, "Organic" and "Conversion to Organic". In China, 'Organic' is a controlled term and it cannot be applied to food unless it is certified organic (Paull 2007).

China has come into the organic stream after the long evolution of the concept elsewhere. In the West organics has evolved over the past ten decades from Rudolf Steiner's 1924 call for a differentiated agriculture, through the development of biodynamic agriculture in the 1930s, Northbourne's manifesto of organic farming of 1940, the founding of IFOAM in 1972, and the development of standards and certification.

China has leapfrogged this evolutionary process which the organics movement has travelled in the West, and biodynamics, the specific practices of organic farming instigated by Rudolf Steiner, have come only recently to China. The purchaser of a 40 acre long neglected farm in China "hopes to show by example a more natural way of farming to the surrounding rice farmers, who use chemicals heavily, as well as providing food to the [Steiner Waldorf] school at which he is a parent" (Watkin 2013: 13).

A policy of Mao Zedong, Communist Party Chairman, was of "Letting a hundred flowers bloom and a hundred schools of thought contend" (quoted by Hubei Museum of Art, 2013). There are high hopes that China will not just adopt organic agriculture in its diverse manifestations, but along the way adapt and develop the practices, including growing, storing, processing, packing, and marketing to suit its own circumstances.

## Organic Australia

Australia was an early adopter of the organics idea. The world's first 'organic' association was the Australian Organic Farming and Gardening Association (AOFGS), founded in 1944. The world's first 'organic' journal by an organics association was the *Organic Farming Digest* which appeared in 1946. The world's first set of organic farming principles was developed and published by the AOFGS (AOFGS, 1952; Paull 2008b).

Australia has ten decades of experience and development of organics dating from 1928 when an Italian artist and farmer, Ernesto Genoni, recently returned to Australia after a decade in Europe, joined the Agricultural Experimental Circle of Anthroposophical Farmers and Gardeners (AECAFG), headquartered at the Goetheanum in Switzerland (Paull 2013). In Europe, Genoni had met with Steiner, stayed at the Goetheanum, and left when Steiner became terminally ill in September 1924. Genoni worked with the leading advocates and practitioners of biodynamic agriculture including Ehrenfried Pfeiffer and Ernst Stegemann (Genoni c.1955).

There have been four waves of the development of organic agriculture on Australia starting with the Anthroposophists in the 1920s and 1930s, The second wave were the organics pioneers of the 1940s and 1950s during which time there was a proliferation of organics advocacy groups, beginning with the AOFGS of 1944, the

Compost Society in Victoria founded in 1945, and the Living Soil Association of Tasmania founded in 1946.

Rachel Carson's book *Silent Spring* injected new life into the organics movement worldwide and the 1960s and 1970s witnessed a wave of disseminators. This period saw the publication of the mass-market mini self-help book *Organic Gardening* by Audrey Windram (1975), and also the first popular organics periodical to achieve national distribution, the *Organic Farmer and Gardener* published by the Organic Gardening and Farming Society of Tasmania (OGFST).

The explosion at the Chernobyl nuclear reactor in Ukraine in 1986 and the worldwide diffusion of radioactive contamination, especially across Europe, focussed the world on the safety of food supply with worldwide restrictions placed on the movement and importation food along with the radiation testing of imported food. Soon after, the National Association for Sustainable Agriculture, Australia (NASAA) and the Biological Farmers of Australia (BFA) (now Australian Organic) were founded, in 1987 and 1988 respectively, and have grown to become Australia's two leading organics certifiers (Paull 2013). Australia hosted the Organic World Congress, IFOAM's triennial conference and showcase of organics research and developments, in Adelaide in 2005. An Australian, Andre Leu, is currently the President of IFOAM.

Australia has long held number one position for the total of certified organic agricultural hectares (12,001,724 ha), well ahead of the second and third place getters, Argentina (3,637,466 ha) and USA (2,178,471 ha) (Willer & Lernoud 2014). The total value of the organic industry in Australia is estimated to be A$1.276b (€855m) (Monk, Mascitelli, Lobo, Chen & Bez 2012). Farm gate sales are estimated at A$329m (€220). The farm gate value is dominated by five categories of product which account for 76 per cent of the total value, namely, beef (22 per cent), fruit (19 per cent), vegetables (18 per cent), dairy (nine per cent), and wool (eight per cent) (derived from Monk et al. 2012). Australian exports of organics are put at A$152 m (€101.6 m) (Willer & Lernoud 2014) and imports at A$220 m (€147 m) (Monk et al. 2012).

The term 'organic' is not controlled in Australia, so the figures for certified organic hectares will underestimate the farms actually practicing organic agriculture. Supermarkets will generally only sell organic products that are certified but such a constraint will generally not apply at farmer's markets. Under fair trading legislation there is a requirement that claims are not false and misleading so goods described as 'organic' by a seller must be thereby accurately described. Australian organic standards can be freely downloaded from the web (but not from the pay-to-view standard sold by Standards Australia) so that a producer can determine that their production practices meet an organic standard.

## Organic opportunities and challenges for Australia and China

The opportunities to grow the 'organic pie' are substantial for both China and Australia. However the challenges and the opportunities are far from identical, although the goals of growing the production area, increasing the market awareness, fostering consumer confidence in certification and labeling, broadening the product offering and availability, and increasing sales are shared issues. Some of the aspects of organics opportunity and challenge are examined below.

### Area

It has been said that the 'room for improvement' is a big room, and it is certainly the case that there are great opportunities for both

Australia and China to grow their organic sectors. Australia has 2.93 per cent of its agricultural land certified as organic as a proportion of its total agricultural land. This is well above the world's 0.86 per cent of agricultural land certified as organic, but it is well below the global leaders of the Falkland Islands (Malvinas) with 36.34 per cent, Liechtenstein with 29.60 per cent, Austria with 19.70 per cent, and thirty other countries rank ahead of Australia. China has 0.36 per cent of its agricultural land certified as organic. This is well below par for the world, and China is outranked on this measure by 86 countries (Willer & Lernoud 2014). The hectarage figures suggest that there is massive potential for growing the organics sectors of both Australia and China.

**Pollution**

"The food is not contaminated and that creates high demand in China" declared Yongbei Tang about produce from Tasmania, Australia's island state (quoted by Hanson 2014: 16). Australians take it for granted that their air is crisp and clean, that their water is safe and drinkable straight from the tap, and that their environment can be fairly described as 'clean and green', and by extension that their food is by and large 'clean and green'. One consequence is that, for most, the imperative for seeking organic food is a somewhat distant imperative, without a pressing in-your-face urgency. This complacency produces something of a brake on the growth of the domestic organics sector. On the other hand, the clean green image of Australia can be harnessed to market Australian produce in export markets.

As the CEO of Apple and Pear Australia Limited (APAL), John Dollisson, recently stated on the occasion of a first shipment of Tasmanian apples to Shanghai: "China is a huge potential market for Australian apples and pears because our fruit has a unique clean, green and safe image that is becoming increasingly popular among high-end consumers in the country" (Acres 2014).

In contrast to the situation in Australia, China has a serious pollution problem, some would say catastrophic, with air pollution frequently at 'hazardous' levels (AQICN, 2014). China has experienced food scares, including fatal events, which have shaken consumer confidence in the safety of the food chain. With palpable pollution evident on a daily basis this creates an impetus to seek unpolluted food. There are three food eco-labelling certification systems in China: certified organic, Green Food, and Hazard-free food (No-harm food) (Paull 2008a). The current pollution levels in China will require nothing less than a massive and protracted effort to remedy, and in the meantime the pollution awareness of consumers can create demand for organic food, subject to price, availability, and consumer awareness of organics.

## Better reportage

Measuring progress and identifying trends relies on accurate valid, reliable and timely data that are regularly reported. The organics data sets for both Australia and China leave much to be desired. The accounts of certified organic agriculture hectares in Australia report the deceptively precise figure of 12,001,724 hectares, unchanged over the past four years (Willer & Kilcher 2011, 2012; Willer & Lernoud 2014; Willer, Lernoud & Kilcher 2013). The corresponding figure for China is reported as 1,900,000 hectares, unchanged for the past two years (Willer & Lernoud 2014; Willer et al. 2013). Australia has not reported the number of organics importers or exporters, and China has not reported producers, processors, importers, or exporters (Willer & Lernoud 2014). Retail sales of organic food in Australia is reported as €927m and in China variously as €791m and over US

$2b (Willer & Lernoud 2014); these figures are best taken as rough estimates or, probably more fairly, as rough guesstimates rather than 'bankable' figures.

## Better engagement

Australia and China are not as engaged with the diversity of the global organics enterprise as some other countries. Neither Australia nor China report any data for organic aquaculture or organic forestry, while the global figures are 33,844 hectares and 44,013 hectares, respectively (Willer & Lernoud 2014). Australia does not report any organic wild collection area, while China reports 982,400 hectares, and the global total figure is a massive 30,359,009 hectares. Forestry is highly contentious activity in Australia, and especially Tasmania. Credible third party certification would be welcomed by many, and why not the gold standard of certified organic forestry?

## Brand

Organics is a sector with weak brand presence. It is a phenomenon that applies in both Australia and China where organic brands lack recognition, market penetration and consumer awareness. This weak brand presence for organics contrasts with, say, cola drinks where in Australia, for example, that space is 'owned' by Coca Cola and Pepsi, with fast food hamburgers where that space is dominated by McDonald's, with breakfast cereals which is dominated by Kellogg's, and chocolate where the space is dominated by Cadbury.

It could be argued that 'organic' is the brand, but that ducks the issue and is proposing that a certification mark take on the role of brand. 'Organic' is ill suited to such a task for which it was never designed. Organic-as-brand sidesteps the important issue that readily identifiable brand marking and livery can deliver consumer loyalty and habituation by simplifying the shopping process and promising a consistent product experience to a consumer, and for neither of which is a certification mark a substitute.

There is the opportunity for organic brands to develop and grow and to stake a claim to some market niche. The challenge in this is exemplified in the case of the Tasmanian organic apple brand, Willie Smith. The brand is new and is currently applied to organic apple cider, as well as the Willie Smith Apple Museum nearby the apple orchard at Grove. But the orchard's organic apples, which are available nationwide at Coles stores, are home branded as "Coles Organic" (Coles 2013). This home-branding strategy has great advantages for a supermarket company which can switch suppliers, leaving consumers none the wiser, as the product branding and livery remains unchanged, and the consumer's loyalty to the product is unwittingly transferred.

**Premium**

Certified organic food sells at a price premium. This is the main impediment for consumers to purchase organic (Nielsen 2005b), and the flip side is that it is a motivating factor for farmers. 'Certified organic' is the gold standard for producing clean food, and so there should be no surprise that certified organic food is priced at a premium. It is the size of the premium that is the issue.

In a study of Australian consumers, respondents valued 'certified organic' at 16 per cent over undifferentiated product (Paull 2009b). Actual price premiums for certified organic in Australia average 80 per cent (Halpin 2004). The price premium needs to capture the costs of certification, the higher labour demands for producing organically where applicable, a lower yield if that is the case, the savings on chemical inputs, and perhaps some reward to the producer for the intrusion of the extra scrutiny and oversight over the production.

There are consumers who are price buyers and will always opt for 'cheapest', and at the other end of the scale there are buyers who are relatively price insensitive, but most purchasers are making price-considered purchasing trade-off decisions most of the time. With a value of 16 per cent to Australian consumers, but frequently with an actual premium over that, this means that the price premium is for many consumers, for much of the time, failing a good value test. It is expected that as the market share increases the premium shrinks.

In China price premiums for certified organic are much greater than in Australia, Europe or North America. For organic fresh vegetables premiums of 206 per cent to 408 per cent are reported (Xu, 2008). Such premiums take the organic option out of the orbit of most potential purchasers, and, given the global experience of organic production, they smack of price gouging. It may be a case of 'charge what the market will bear', and there are also issues, such as that the market for certified organic in China is still an immature market, that certification may be cumbersome, and that the choice of retail outlets are limited. Nevertheless, it is a reasonable expectation that organic premiums in China will drop to more manageable proportions and fall back to the 0-100 per cent range that we witness elsewhere in the world. And, hand in hand with shrinking premiums, we can expect to see rising sales.

## Logo

China has had a mandated national logo for organic since 2005, and this is a desirable state of affairs which enables a consumer to readily identify an organic product. Imported organic products to China must also bear the Chinese organic logo which serves as an aid to consumer identification of organic. The logo is bilingual, Chinese and English, and that is most helpful for the expat community and visitors within China, and also helpful where Chinese organic products are exported.

The Chinese organic logo is itself rather odd, a cross between a stylized Saturn with rings and a football passing through a hoop. The logic of the graphic escapes the present author and is equally elusive to the Chinese shoppers, sales staff, and others whom I have asked. By way of contrast, there is also a standardized Green Food logo. It is readily identifiable, is also bilingual (but not always), is coloured green which is logical, and the graphic element of the logo is of a stylized plant, all of which fits nicely with the intent of the certification.

Australia has a proliferation of organic logos. Each certifier has their own logo. The most commonly seen are, firstly, the Organic Australia 'bud' logo, bearing the text "Australian Certified Organic" with a stylized germinating plant, and secondly, the NASAA logo with text "Certified Organic" and two leaves. The Australian Government issued a national logo, which was radioactive-orange in colour and altogether quite ghastly; it bears no discernible salience with the organic brand, the word 'organic' is entirely absent, and the uptake of which was voluntary and appears to have faltered, which can only be described as 'for the best'.

A national logo was the right decision for China where there was an uncontrolled proliferation of logos and which was confusing and corroding trust. Europe has adopted a compulsory logo which has no text at all, so it is best to be a mind reader. It is a green star-spangled banner which was chosen by a committee from a public competition. It can be described as a weak logo which appears to have mislaid its core message someplace, and whether it is an indictment of committees or competitions cannot be stated without more data.

A national logo for Australia that could appear alongside existing certifier logos might be a worthwhile idea to collectively identify the diversity of organic produce. On the other hand, no logo is better than a poor logo, committees and competitions may be fraught, either or both, and there is currently no imperative for a common logo in Australia.

## Consumer awareness

It is probably fair to say that, in China, consumer awareness of pollution and food scares is high while awareness of organics is low. News of food scandals spreads rapidly, even in a totalitarian society, bad news sells newspapers, whereas the organics message is a harder sell. In marketing there is a maxim that people will do more to avoid a loss than make a gain. Chinese consumers (N=94) are more likely to purchase Green Food if they were young (under 25 years) or well educated (completed College or University) (Wang, Xiang & Xing 2013), and the same may very well apply to organics purchasers.

Some supermarkets in China, for example the Carrefour chain, display explanatory banners of text and graphics outlining the organic difference and extolling the benefits. Some supermarkets have in-store promotional displays, for example for organic dairy products which are dressed up as luxury goods with elaborate packaging, and may be accompanied by promotional staff. Green Food is more familiar to Chinese consumers and is more readily available. For awareness raising and the promotion of Green Food it has been suggested that TV and radio be used, and that "public organizations should cooperate with producers in holding public benefit activities" (Wang et al. 2013: i). For the promotion of organic food in China, "There is a need to clearly explain the meaning of the term 'organic' … Educational campaigns need to be organised to raise awareness of and clarify the term 'organic'" (Chen 2012: 210).

The United Arab Emirates (UAE) have recently reported success with an organics awareness raising amongst consumers. "The organic food market in the United Arab Emirates is booming and supply cannot meet demand ... The growing demand for organic food is due to a number of reasons: one of them being that the Ministry of Environment and Water has launched awareness programs addressing organic farming ... Moreover the ministry launched a number of organic farmers markets to not only help farmers sell their products but also to increase awareness among consumers about organic food" (AlShara 2014: 181). The UAE market has similarities to the Chinese market in that, in both, 'organic' is a relatively new idea and it is a foreign idea – although the idea of healthful and wholesome food is already very familiar and the populations are already very food-aware, and the UAE has adopted a bilingual organics logo, in Arabic and English.

The essence of an awareness raising program is: tell them and they will buy. The message needs to include the points of difference, and the benefits need to be explained so that they outweigh the off-putting price premium.

An awareness raising strategy in Australia is the introduction of the Organic School Gardens Program. It has received funding from the Victorian Department of Education and Early Childhood Development and is underwritten by BFA Ltd. (Monk et al., 2012). The idea is not a new one, it was proposed in Australia by the founder of the Living Soil Association of Tasmania, Henry Shoobridge, in 1944 (Paull 2009a). Organic school gardens is a simple idea that appears worthy of expansion to all schools – not only in Australia but why not also in China and, in fact, where is the country that would not benefit from such a program?

## Provenance and transparency

For a certification system to credibly work it requires traceability – and organics certification is a mature certification system that incorporates traceability. But, and it is a big but, this traceability is data tightly held by the certifier and often veiled or concealed from the consumer, which is convenient for all parties other than the consumer who is left in the dark.

The game proceeds like this: organic produce is sourced in a low cost market, say China. Australian retailers are aware that Australian consumers value down, and may avoid altogether, food from China, for example nominating food scares as their reason (Paull 2009b). The product is certified by an Australian certifier, frequently by Organic Australia, and that scores it an "Australian Certified Organic" logo which will then appear prominently on the front of the pack. Meanwhile, on the back of the pack, a consumer may get lucky and find "Product of China", but frequently will find nothing more informative than "Packed in Australia from imported ingredients" or some such attribution which dupes the consumer, even if it may not trigger a claim of being false and misleading under the Trade Practices Act.

For China where consumers have suffered too many local food scandals, and are somewhat wary of the integrity of current local production methods, "imported" is a valued attribution on food products, but this is not the case in Australia for Australian consumers.

The organic sector relies on consumer trust. There is a premium to be paid, that is almost a given, and the certification logo attests this added value of the product. The logo is the only tangible indicator of the added value, since a consumer cannot tell an organic from a chemical product by the look and feel. To make an informed choice, and to not be gypped, the consumer needs the provenance data. We may have political reasons for boycotting the goods of a country, for example, or we may value up some countries products and value down others on the basis of the provenance and quite independently of the organic claim. The consumer is entitled to know what the certifier knows, data that would impact on the consumer purchase choice were it known. At present in Australia, it appears that even the weak provenance labeling prescribed by the Government is flouted; examples can be found in any major Australian supermarket selling organic labeled foods. This is a scandal in the making, and an opportunity to do better, and while this shoddy behavior persists it damages the good standing of the organics sector.

## Transnational processing

Australia has, on the one hand, the advantage of having arguably the best growing environment for organic food in the world and, on the other hand, the disadvantages of having some of the highest wages in the world, along with a small market. In contrast, China has some of the world's most polluted air, water, and soil for growing, but abundant cheap labour with sound food and agriculture skills, and a massive market. When we add to this mix of comparative advantages and disadvantages, the fact that travel and transport are cheaper, easier and more reliable than they have ever been, the scene is set for the potential of transnational food.

Transnational food is food where food has made three or more national stops in the production, processing, and sales, and so it goes beyond 'imported ingredients'. Local food is (in the broadest definition) where food is produced and sold within a single country (for example "Product of Australia" which is sold in Australia). Imported food is where food is produced in one country (or several) and sold in another (for example "Product of Italy" sold in Australia or China). An example of the emergence of transnational food, is cashew nuts grown in Australia (Northern Queensland where the growing conditions are right and the environment is clean), they are shipped to Vietnam where they are dehusked (using low-cost skilled labour) (Straight 2011), and they are shipped back to be sold in Australia as "Product of Australia". This has the advantage of generating work for skilled low wage Vietnamese food processing workers. The downside is that those consumers who are purchasing on the basis of 'food miles' are deceived into imagining that these cashews have travelled from an Australian farm to them somewhat directly, and certainly not transnationally. While there is the option for a producer to state on the pack: "Product of Australia" and "Processed in Vietnam" there appears to be no requirement to do that (FSANZ 2006) and it is unlikely to achieve a marketing benefit, quite the contrary, a fact of which marketers will be well aware. This is a shortcoming, among many, of the food provenance labeling in Australia, which often conceals more than it reveals, and it presents an opportunity for improvement.

Australia has the capacity to expand its agricultural production, especially organic, while China is witnessing a shift of rural population to urban areas. This offers opportunities for food growing in Australia, then food processing and transformation in China, and food marketing whereever. To achieve organic certification on the end product, all stages of the growing and processing must be under organic certification. That is why some products in Australia, for example, will state "grown organically" or "grown biodynamically"; they may lack organic certification because the processing facility was not organically certified. As transnational food production becomes more nuanced, the provenance labeling prescriptions need to evolve to keep pace and reflect the new realities, and thereby maintain the trust of consumers who care to know where their food has been.

## Green food

Green Food is a Chinese eco-agricultural innovation of the Ministry of Agriculture and dates from 1990. Green Food is a step down from organic agriculture and a step up from full-blown chemical agriculture. There are four environmental criteria for Green Food certification: good air quality, good quality water and soil, drinking quality water for processing, and reduced and restricted synthetic fertilizers and pesticides. Two grades of Green Food, Grade A and Grade AA allow for a guided and controlled pathway to organic production and certification.

An inventory of China's agricultural land reported 3.1 million hectares as organic, 10 million hectares as Green Food, and 21.1 million hectares as Hazard-free (Paull 2008a). This puts China at the forefront of global eco-food labeling, with the total hectares under China's three eco-labeling schemes (34.2 m ha) being comparable to the world's total under organic agriculture certification (37.5 m ha) (Paull 2008a; Willer & Lernoud 2014).

The area under Green Food certification in China is more than three times the area under organic certification. This offers a large reserve pool of farming land and farmers that have a history of third party scrutiny and certification, and which can progress, with some adjustments to their production and oversight practices, along the path to organic certification. The triggers for such a progression may kick in when the incentives are right, perhaps government incentives, rising consumer demand, or improved marketing and distribution opportunities, including export opportunities. Green Food puts China is a unique position to have a large pool of farmers and farm land well on the way to being 'organic-ready'. Green Food is reported as more frequently purchased by younger (<25 years) and better educated (College or university educated) Chinese consumers (Wang et al. 2013) and these are potential target demographics to also engage with organic food.

## Free trade

Australia signed free trade agreements with Japan and Korea in April 2014 (DFAT 2014), and a free trade agreement between Australia and China is currently under negotiation. Such an agreement has the potential to facilitate the flow of organic food between the two countries. Australian organic product entering China needs to be certified to China's organic standard and bear China's organic logo. The situation has been described as follows: "The Chinese market, while offering great future potential for Australian businesses, has more recently made growth difficult due to regulatory and standards divergences ... specific market requirements, including additional certification requirements, are adding cost and complexity to exporters interested in serving this market" (Monk et al. 2012: 11).

These challenges have been substantially addressed by NASAA, a leading Australian organics certifier, which recently concluded an agreement with a Chinese certifier. "The agreement was signed in Adelaide between NASAA Certified Organic and Beijing WuYue HuaXia Management and Technique Centre (CHC). This is the first time a foreign organization has been approved to inspect organic products for export to China as well as to certify Chinese organic operators to USDA NOP and Japanese Agricultural Standards in China" (Abad 2014: 1).

Chinese organic produce exported to Australia appears to generally have been exported in bulk and packaged in Australia, certified by an Australian certifier, and, it seems, most commonly by Australian Certified Organic (ACO). The drawback of this practice is that the ACO logo typically appears prominently on the front of the packaging, while the provenance declaration of "Product of China" or the opaque and reprehensible "Packed in Australia from imported ingredients" appears on the rear, as mini-text and buried in a forest of other text. Australian consumers deserve better.

Australian boutique organic producers, such as Willie Smith organic apple cider and Mole Creek organic leatherwood honey, can benefit from easier access to the Chinese market. These are premium organic products with a very modest premium (in the Australian market) that can showcase the taste and terroir of Tasmania, in particular, and Australia in general. A boost in demand for their products along with their continuing successes can entice other orchardists and apiarists to convert their own operations to organic using, for example, Willie Smith and Mole Creek as exemplars.

## Conclusion

China's Premier Li Keqiang recently declared a "war on pollution" and this was quickly followed by the passing of the long awaited Environmental Protection Law (EPL) on 24 April 2014, and which comes into force in 2015. The new environmental law has been in the drafting and amendment process since 2001 (Jianqiang 2014) and it replaces the previous weak version of 1989. These fresh developments are cause for optimism and bode well for the future of China which is currently burdened with the world's worst pollution and is urgently in need of a successful "war on pollution" (Wubbeke 2014). China's State Council has announced an unprecedented move to address air-pollution with an action plan costing 1.7 trillion yuan (A$293m, €196m) with similar action plans promised for water and soil pollution (Lin 2014).

Organic agriculture has a role to play in reducing China's soil, water, air, and produce pollution. China's new EPL and the declared "war on pollution" can be instruments to refocus farmers, consumers, and administrative authorities that organic agriculture is an 'off the shelf' tool to help China along the path to a cleaner and greener future. Visitors to China are noticing that the most obvious index of pollution, air pollution, is worsening from visit to visit. The tide needs to turn. A dirtier and browner future for China does not bear thinking about. An opinion poll conducted by China Youth Daily put environment as the public's number one concern (Lin 2014). The continuing uptake of organic agriculture offers real environmental dividends, and is a move in the right direction.

By way of contrast, in Australia there is little compelling pressure to increase organic production. There is a lack of food scares. There is a lack of engagement of the media with pesticide issues which are, of their very nature, multifaceted, somewhat complex and convoluted, and rely on scientific and philosophic perspectives that do not lend themselves to ten-second sound bites and nor to light writing or light reading. Added to this there is no push from the organic sector or the government to inform the public or proselytize on behalf of the organics sector. Australian organic farmers, producers and manufacturers continue to sing their own praises with the sound button turned to mute, or nearly so.

A surety of price premiums, the awareness of success stories, and increasing consumer demand from home or abroad, can potentially drive the Australian organics enterprise forward. There has been considerable chatter that Australia, and even Tasmania, can be the "food bowl of Asia" but such talk is mostly hocus-pocus springing from bogus analysis and wishful thinking. More likely, and more plausibly, is that Australia can provide a premium food platter for Asia. No matter what efficiencies are put in place, there is the stark reality that Australian labour is some of the most expensive in the world. A consequence is that Australia can move away from selling commodities and competing on price, and shift into the premium food space and compete on quality. Embracing this new reality can be a boon for the growth of organics, especially as Asian consumers become more savvy and discerning, as well as more cashed up.

Alongside the upbeat rhetoric of foreseen food exports to China with which newspapers and politicians regale us, Australian producers always need to bear in mind that China can feed itself. It has more than a thousand farmers for every one in Australia. China has a great depth of farming expertise, and farmers who can draw on a history of millennia of sound ecological agriculture. China has one of the great food cuisines of the world and its population has a deep food culture. China can feed itself, farm itself, and with the right will, can lead the world in organic agriculture, and even enjoy some organic delicacies and premium foods from Australia in the process.

## Acknowledgment

This chapter evolved from a presentation at Huazhong Agriculture University, Wuhan (华中农业大学, 武汉，中国) as China – Australia: Organic Opportunities (中国 – 澳大利亚: 有机=机) at the Knowledge Exchange of Quality Food Production and Distribution: China and Australia. The forum was co-hosted by Huazhong Agricultural University and Swinburne University of Technology. The author acknowledges the invitation of Professor Qing Ping, Dean, College of Economics & Management, and the kind hospitality of the International Academic Exchange Center at Huazhong Agricultural University, Wuhan, Hubei Province, China.

## References

Abad, J. (2014). China trade pact to deliver $100m boost to Australian organic producers. Adelaide: National Association for Sustainable Agriculture, Australia (NASAA). Press release 17 March.

Acres. (2014). China receives first shipment of Australian apples. Acres Australia, www.acresaustralia.com.au 12 April.

AlShara, S. M. (2014). The organic farming sector of the United Arab Emirates. In H. Willer & J. Lernoud (Eds.). *The World of Organic Agriculture: Statistics and Emerging Trends 2014* (pp. 180-182). Frick & Bonn: Research Institute of Organic Agriculture (FiBL) & International Federation of Organic Agriculture Movements (IFOAM).

AOFGS. (1952). The Purpose and Objectives of the Australian Organic Farming and Gardening Society Farm & Garden Digest (incorporating Organic Farming Digest), 3(1), 39-40.

AQICN. (2014). Air Pollution in China: Real-time Air Quality Index Visual Map. Beijing: Air Quality Index China (aqicn.org).

Associated Press. (2009). China executes Zhang Yujun, Geng Jinping for roles in deadly tainted milk powder scandal. *Daily News*, 24 November.

Chen, J. (2012). A study investigating the deteminants of consumer buying behavoiur relating to the purchase of organic food products in urban China. PhD thesis. Swinburne University of Technology, Melbourne.

Chevriot, R. (1972). Subject: Creation of an international Federation. Typescript letter, 1 page, undated. Paris: Nature et Progrès.

Coles. (2013). Coles Organic. Melbourne: Coles Supermarkets Australia (coles. com.au).

DFAT. (2014). Australia's Trade Agreements. Canberra: Department of Foreign Affairs and Trade.

FAO. (2014a). Countries: Australia. Rome: Food and Agriculture Organization of the United Nations (FAO).

FAO. (2014b). Countries: China. Rome: Food and Agriculture Organization of the United Nations (FAO).

FAOSTAT. (2014a). Country Profile: Australia. Rome: Food and Agriculture Organization of the United Nations (FAO).

FAOSTAT. (2014b). Country Profile: China. Rome: Food and Agriculture Organization of the United Nations (FAO).

FSANZ. (2006). Country of Origin Food Labelling. Canberra: Food Standards Australia New Zealand (FSANZ).

Genoni, E. (c.1955). Personal memoir, handwritten manuscript, notebook. Private collection.

Giovannucci, D. (2005). Organic Agriculture and Poverty Reduction in Asia: China and India Focus (Report No. 1664). Rome: International Fund fot Agricultural Development (IFAD).

Halpin, D. (2004). *The Australian Organic Industry: A Profile*. Canberra: Department of Agriculture, Fisheries and Forestry.

Hanson, R. (2014). Tassie's China prime time. *The Mercury*, 14, 16 April.

Hubei Museum of Art. (2013). Introduction. Wuhan: Hubei Museum of Art.

Jianqiang, L. (2014). China's new environmental law looks good on paper. *Chinadialogue*, 24 April (www.chinadialogue.net).

King, F. H. (1911). Farmers of Forty Centuries, or Permanent Agriculture in China, Korea and Japan (Edited by Professor J.P. Bruce). Madison, Wisconsin: Mrs. F. H. King.

King, F. H. (2011). Farmers of Forty Centuries or Permanent Agriculture in China, Korea and Japan (trans.) (First Chinese language edition; translators: Cheng Cunwang and Shi Yan; translation of the English language book of 1911). Beijing: Oriental Press.

Latner, K., & Lei, A. (2006). Peoples Republic of China, Tomatoes and Products. GAIN Report, No. Ch6024, USDA Foreign Agricultural Service, 15 May.

Li, S. (2005). Agricultural mechanization promotion in China – current situation and future. *CIGR Journal of Scientific Research and Development*, VII, 1-17.

Lin, L. (2014). Is China underfunding its 'war on pollution'? *Chinadialogue*, 17 March (www.chinadialogue.net).

McKinna, D. (2006). Export potential for organics, opportunities and barriers. Canberra: Rural Industries Research and Development Corporation (RIRDC).

Monk, A., Mascitelli, B., Lobo, A., Chen, J., & Bez, N. (2012). *Australian Organic Market Report.* Brisbane: Biological Farmers of Australia (BFA).

Nielsen. (2005a). *Consumer attitudes towards organic foods, A global consumer survey*: ACNielsen.

Nielsen. (2005b). Functional Foods & Organics: A global AC Nielsen online survey on consumer behaviour and attitudes: ACNielsen.

Northbourne, Lord. (1940). *Look to the Land.* London: Dent.

Paull, J. (2006). The farm as organism: the foundational idea of organic agriculture. *Journal of Bio-Dynamics Tasmania*, (80), 14-18.

Paull, J. (2007). China's organic revolution. Journal of Organic Systems, 2(1), 1-11.

Paull, J. (2008a). The greening of China's food – green food, organic food and eco-labelling. Paper presented at the Sustainable Consumption and Alternative Agri-Food Systems Conference (SUSCONS).

Paull, J. (2008b). The lost history of organic farming in Australia. *Journal of Organic Systems*, 3(2), 2-17.

Paull, J. (2009a). The Living Soil Association: Pioneering organic farming and innovating social inclusion. *Journal of Organic Systems*, 4(1), 15-33.

Paull, J. (2009b). *The Value of Eco-Labelling: Price premiums & consumer valuations of organic, natural, and place of origin food labels.* Saarbrücken, Germany: VDM Verlag.

Paull, J. (2010). From France to the World: The International Federation of Organic Agriculture Movements (IFOAM). *Journal of Social Research & Policy*, 1(2), 93-102.

Paull, J. (2011a). Attending the first organic agriculture course: Rudolf Steiner's Agriculture Course at Koberwitz, 1924. *European Journal of Social Sciences*, 21(1), 64-70.

Paull, J. (2011b). The Betteshanger Summer School: Missing link between biodynamic agriculture and organic farming. *Journal of Organic Systems*, 6(2), 13-26.

Paull, J. (2011c). Biodynamic Agriculture: The journey from Koberwitz to the World, 1924-1938. *Journal of Organic Systems*, 6(1), 27-41.

Paull, J. (2011d). The making of an agricultural classic: Farmers of Forty Centuries or Permanent Agriculture in China, Korea and Japan, 1911-2011. *Agricultural Sciences*, 2(3), 175-180.

Paull, J. (2011e). Organics Olympiad 2011: Global Indices of Leadership in Organic Agriculture. *Journal of Social and Development Sciences*, 1(4), 144-150.

Paull, J. (2011f). The uptake of organic agriculture: A decade of worldwide development. *Journal of Social and Development Sciences*, 2(3), 111-120.

Paull, J. (2012). Organics Olympiad 2012: Global Indices of Leadership in Organic Agriculture. *Organic News*, 26 July, 2 August, 9 August.

Paull, J. (2013). A history of the organic agriculture movement in Australia. In B. Mascitelli & A. Lobo (Eds.). *Organics in the Global Food Chain* (pp. 37-60). Ballarat: Connor Court Publishing.

People's Daily. (2001). Central economic working conference held November 27 to 29. *Peoples Daily*, Beijing, 30 November, <english.people.com.cn>.

Pfeiffer, E. (1938). *Bio-Dynamic Farming and Gardening: Soil Fertility Renewal and Preservation* (F. Heckel, Trans.). New York: Anthroposophic Press.

Smil, V. (2001). *Enriching the Earth: Fritz Haber, Carl Bosch, and the Transformation of World Food Production.* Cambridge, USA: The MIT Press.

Steiner, R. (1924). The Agricultural Course ("Printed for private circulation only", 1938 ed, new translation, translator not identified). London: Rudolf Steiner Publishing.

Straight, K. (2011). Is there cash in cashews? ABC *Landline*, 18 March.

Wang, S., Xiang, L., & Xing, F. (2013). Green food development in China. Bachelor thesis: Kristianstad University, Sweden.

Watkin, D. (2013). Magic water – the Biodynamic message in China. *Journal for Anthroposophy in Australia*, 3, 13-14.

WHO. (2008). Children's health in the environment. Geneva: World Health Organization.

Willer, H., & Kilcher, L. (Eds.). (2011). *The World of Organic Agriculture: Statistics and Emerging Trends 2011*: Bonn: International Federation of Organic Agriculture Movements (IFOAM); Frick, Switzerland: Research Institute of Organic Agriculture (FiBL).

Willer, H., & Kilcher, L. (Eds.). (2012). *The World of Organic Agriculture: Statistics and Emerging Trends 2012*: Bonn: International Federation of Organic Agriculture Movements (IFOAM); Frick, Switzerland: Research Institute of Organic Agriculture (FiBL).

Willer, H., & Lernoud, J. (Eds.). (2014). *The World of Organic Agriculture: Statistics and Emerging Trends 2014*: Frick, Switzerland: Research Institute of Organic Agriculture (FiBL) & Bonn: International Federation of Organic Agriculture Movements (IFOAM).

Willer, H., Lernoud, J., & Kilcher, L. (Eds.). (2013). *The World of Organic Agriculture: Statistics and Emerging Trends 2013*: Frick, Switzerland: Research Institute of Organic Agriculture (FiBL) & Bonn: International Federation of Organic Agriculture Movements (IFOAM).

Windram, A. (1975). *Organic Gardening.* Adelaide: Rigby

World Bank. (2014). *Fertilizer consumption.* Washington: World Bank Group.

Wubbeke, J. (2014). The three-year battle for China's new environmental law. *Chinadialogue*, 25 April (www.chinadialogue.net).

Xu, F. (2008). *Shanghai Organic Retail Market Profile* (GAIN Report # CH8821). Shanghai: USDA Foreign Agricultural Service.

Zhang, W., Jiang, F., & Ou, J. (2011). *Global pesticide consumption and pollution: with China as a focus.* Proceedings of the International Academy of Ecology and Environmental Sciences, 1(2), 125-144.

Zong, H. (2002). The Role of Agriculture and Rural Development in China. In *Organic Agriculture and Rural Poverty Alleviation, Potential and Best Practices in Asia.* Bangkok: United Nations Economic and Social Commission for Asia and the Pacific (UNESCAP).

# 4

# From farm to fork: Designing more coherent national and transnational food regulation

**Jo En Yap, Benedict Sheehy and Donald Feaver**

## Introduction

The most fundamental of all the challenges facing humanity is how to provide enough healthy food to meet the needs of the planet's current and future inhabitants. It is one of those challenges that is both global and local in scope. The magnitude of the challenge is evident in both the number of problems and their ripple effects which go in all directions though the supply-chains that provides food. At the supply end, issues such as effective land use, water pollution, soil contamination, erosion, pest adaptation and resistance are prevalent (Foster et al. 2006). Economic concerns that affect entire supply-chains include mounting fuel and transportation costs and the shifting loci of power to monopolistic, vertically integrated corporate actors that increasingly dictate the composition and content of those supply-chains (Kaditi 2013). At the consumption end of supply-chains, social issues such as rising prices, food deserts, health and safety issues, malnutrition, obesity, micronutrient deficiencies and other non-communicable diseases also abound (Viola et al. 2013).

Over the last several decades, policy-makers and researchers have tended to deal with these, and other problems using what is known as the divide-and-conquer approach. This approach takes large, multi-faceted problems and breaks them down into smaller, individual components. While it is "human nature to reduce a problem into solvable parts" (Muller et al. 2009: 238), the divide-and-conquer approach has not been effective as evidenced by the increasing issues affecting the food system which have only grown in magnitude using that approach. An alternative to the divide-and-conquer approach is the more contemporary systems approach. A systems approach seeks to better understand the complex interactions between humans and the natural systems within which we live. It recognizes that many problems are interrelated and seeks to construct analytical frameworks that better connect numerous competing problems with and between the various actors involved in the food system as well as to each other (Block et al. 2011; Ericksen 2008; Neff et al. 2009; Sobal et al. 1998).

A systems approach, however, is problematic in a neo-liberal policy environment. Whereas a systems approach takes multiple actors, multi-environments and dynamics as a starting point, neo-liberal governance models narrowly focus on individuals: individual choice, individual accountability and linear metrics. It ignores the complexities of the social interactions that animate the food system as a whole. Regulators operating within the neo-liberal governance paradigm are usually restricted, by statutory mandates, from investigating and responding to the individual-society dynamic or the socio-physical factors that influence how food is produced, processed, distributed, and consumed. That is, statutes are usually drafted to deal with specific discrete issues with carefully delimited scope and powers. Given that such conventional regulatory approaches are not developed within, and hence unable to address complex dynamic systems, it is clear that new approaches to solving and regulating the problems of a food system composed as it is of innumerable institutional and physical environments that are increasingly transnational in nature is needed.

To the extent that some nations have attempted to tackle the coordination problems associated with national food systems, the divide-and-conquer approach still seems to dominate policy perceptions, framings, as well as the design of policy and statutory frameworks intended to bring greater order and coherence to the food system. The basic shortcoming of this approach is that the broad objective of better policy coordination is lost among competing interests and improperly chosen policy objectives. For example, Australia's recent attempts to fashion a national food strategy appear to have missed the mark completely. Rather than approaching the food system as a social coordination problem encompassing a range of important social, economic and environmental challenges, the strategy focuses primarily on the economic opportunities that food production and export hold for Australia. This economic aspect of the food system, though important, should not be viewed as the primary objective of a national strategy that should, instead, be designed to balance more fundamental concerns such as environmental sustainability, public health and safety as well as the viability of primary producers and the communities within which they live.

The objective of this paper is to discuss how a new theoretical approach to designing regulation might better coordinate and manage the multiple competing actors, environments and problems affecting the food system. The question investigated is whether this approach more coherently connects issues, problems and actors involved in the production, processing, distribution and consumption of food, leading to better (i.e. economically and environmentally sustainable and healthy) outcomes. The generality of the investigation requires an equally general unit of analysis—the food system as whole, rather than discrete portions and specific problems. The paper begins with a discussion of the divide-and-conquer approach. This section is followed by brief discussion of the systems approach, the approach that has gained much traction in recent times. Next, a discussion of the theory underpinning the proposed alternative regulatory framework, the theory of coherent regulation, is presented. This is followed by a discussion of how the numerous problems affecting the food system can be more coherently ordered, connected and coordinated in a manner that provides a foundation for a coherent policy and strategy with which to guide the regulation of the food system as a whole. This paper concludes with a discussion of the implications of the proposed framework and directions for future research.

## The divide-and-conquer approach

As noted in the introduction, the dominant method—the divide-and-conquer approach—takes large and complex problems and attempts to break them down into smaller, more manageable 'bite-sized' chunks. Each chunk is typically managed by the actor(s) most affected by and closest to the problem being addressed. For example, public health actors have assumed, among other things, primary responsibility for combating the obesity epidemic by developing policies, regulatory interventions and programs aimed at encouraging healthy behaviour (Scammon et al. 2011; Harris et al. 2009), promoting better eating decisions and habits (Finkelstein et al. 2004), educating society about the health benefits of physical activity (Pratt et al. 2004) and creating healthier eating environments (Shill et al. 2011). Actors further up the food supply chain, such as food producers and manufacturers, are more concerned about food (in)security issues and economic viability concerns. Actions taken by these actors are directed towards increasing efficiencies and crop and animal production yields (and hence, the quantity and availability of food). Ensuring a prosperous economic environment for primary producers and processors is a key priority (Muller et al. 2009; Wallinga 2009; Wallinga, Schoonover & Muller 2009). Other actors, such as environmental activists and agronomists focus on environmental sustainability concerns. These actors seek to influence the policy debate surrounding problems such as climate change, land use, soil and water pollution and biodiversity concerns (Ericksen, Ingram & Liverman 2009; Lichtfouse et al. 2009).

The divide-and-conquer approach has had some positive outcomes. However, the frictions between environmental, economic and social problems plaguing the food system persist. The weaknesses of the divide-and-conquer approach can be summarized as follows. First, by reducing complex problems into smaller solvable parts, actors become segmented and confined to their respective silos/domains. These silos prevent them from coordinating with other food system participants. Regulatory interventions then have a tendency to be designed in a manner that advances independent goals and agendas. While having clear and specific policy objectives are essential, the downside is that policy is fashioned without regard for the food system as a whole (Muller et al. 2009). Often, decisions designed to advance one actor's goals are made on the basis of short-term gains (Brownson, Fielding & Maylahn 2009). Operating within the confines of silos/domains and pursuing independent goals can result in the loss of many opportunities to coordinate the actions of the various actors and align the policy objectives that might address problems in a more holistic manner (Ericksen, Ingram & Liverman 2009).

Second, the single actor focus of the divide-and-conquer approach tends to allow goals and agendas to be pursued by one actor which may be incompatible with another's. As a result, regulation intended to solve one actor's problem or advance one actor's goals leads to unintended consequences in the domain(s) of others (Muller et al. 2009). In the systems literature, this is known as the ripple effect (Wallinga et al. 2009). Instances of the ripple effect within the food system are well documented (Harvie 2006; Jackson et al. 2009; Muller et al. 2009; Wallinga 2009). For example, to increase the quantity of food produced at cheaper prices, industrial farmers began to extensively use pesticide, fertilizers and water as well as the farming practices of fast crop rotations and monoculture. While these practices have advanced the goal of reducing hunger and food insecurity, these positive effects are counterbalanced by negative environmental effects such as soil erosion, water pollution and contamination of the water supply, chemical and pesticide resistant weeds, pests and diseases (Lichtfouse et al. 2009). Another example of the ripple effect is the cheap commodity policy (i.e., where the production of corn, soybean and other low-cost commodities are subsidized). Although this policy benefits actors involved in agribusiness and manufacturing, these benefits are offset by the negative effects felt by downstream actors. Negative effects include the an increase in the amount of processed and fast foods and their provision at a cost advantage compared to fresh produce and healthier foods (Wallinga et al. 2009).

The existence of incompatible goals not only indirectly leads to negative consequences for other actors and negates the effectiveness of other policies, initiatives and interventions; it can also create positive feedback loops (Erickson et al. 2009; Kreuter et al. 2004; Meadows 1999). For example, the increase in the use of pesticides places pressure on natural selection forces and processes (i.e., the evolution of pesticide and chemical resistant pest and diseases). To combat this, greater quantities of pesticides and chemicals need to be used (Harvie 2006). These examples illustrate the frictions that can arise as a result of incompatible goals when they are examined and managed in isolation. Domain-specific policies developed to advance domain-specific goals often introduce unintended consequences in the form of new vulnerabilities that give rise to new problems. To a certain degree, this phenomenon of unintended consequences has made some parties hesitant to regulate at all, and perhaps rightly so where the regulatory approaches are the limited neoliberal approaches. The problem is that the default of unregulated food supply becomes a free-for-all dominated by the most powerful—hardly a guide for safe, sustainable, healthy food.

Third, power imbalances are endemic in the food system. When regulation is designed with limited attention to the system as a whole and focused primarily on individual actors, it is no surprise that when putting forward recommendations and implement policies, actors operating in one area are opposed by actors from another area (Brownson, Fielding & Maylahn 2009). One set of actors may have more influence and resources to promote their goals and agendas as compared to others. For example, Bonanno and Constance (2001) examine transnational corporations' (TNCs) use of political and economic power to influence and bypass state rules and regulations and to counteract resistance from local communities to advance their interests. In a review of regulatory interventions designed to promote healthy food environments, Shill and colleagues (2011) examined the conflict between public agencies' objectives and policies and found that the most powerful actors involved in the policy-making process are inclined to place economic considerations above public health considerations. Importantly, it was observed that policies aimed at improving diet quality and prevent over-consumption (such as the reduction of portion sizes and the reformulation of food and beverage products) tend to target actors involved in food marketing and service as opposed to actors involved in primary production, manufacturing, distribution and retail (Shill et al. 2011). This policy focus, in part, results from powerful actors who have the resources to use the media and as a result, are influential in shaping public perceptions and demands than are the less visible downstream actors. As a result, policies are usually designed and implemented at the level of least conflict and resistance from the politician's point of view. To use Meadow's (1999) terminology, policy is directed at the level of constants, parameters and numbers. While interventions at the level of constants, parameters and numbers are without a doubt the easiest to implement, they have minimal impact and are the least effective in producing long-term significant change (Meadows 1999).

The preceding discussion identifies how the divide-and-conquer approach is not the most appropriate method for dealing with complex problems involved in and confronting the food system. Such an approach is more suitable to tame problems—problems with clearly defined and limited issues and solutions, easily identifiable outcomes that are relatively static and are not expected alter much over time (Hamm 2009; Kreuter et al. 2004; Rittel & Webber 1973).

Far from being tame, the problems plaguing the food system are more accurately described as wicked problems. Wicked problems are elusive and difficult to define. In solving them, it is difficult to determine and agree upon the parameters of the problem, the desired outcomes, measures and methods. This disagreement occurs because the 'best' solution is likely to vary depending on the perspective taken and the associated biases of each actor (e.g., health, ecological, production, retail) involved in the debate. These frictions are further exacerbated by the nature of the problem, where proposed solutions and desired outcomes are influenced by ever-changing social, cultural, economic, political, environmental and technological factors (Hamm 2009; Kreuter et al. 2004; Rittel & Webber 1973). Furthermore, the concerns and issues that make up the problem of the food system are interdependent. They neither occur in isolation nor do they interact in a linear fashion (Malhi et al. 2009). Recognizing the limitations of the divide-and-conquer approach in dealing with the wicked problem inherent in the characteristics of the food system, an alternative approach for understanding and dealing with the range of problems affecting the food system has been proposed: the systems approach.

## The systems approach

In recent years, researchers have increasingly advocated a broader, more holistic approach for understanding and managing the food system (see for example Harvie 2006; Lang 2009; Lichtfouse et al. 2009; Muller et al. 2009; Neff et al. 2009; Story, Hamm & Wallinga 2009a, 2009b; Trochim et al. 1996; Wallinga 2009; Wallinga Schoonover & Muller 2009). Systems theorists have begun conceptualizing the food system as complex set of resources, actor linkages and relationships, in a manner that not only better identifies systemic interdependencies but provides insights into how systemic frictions can be reduced through a better balancing and hence coordination of interests (Malhi et al. 2009). Understanding the food system as interconnected provides a clearer sense of the 'big picture' and enables the various challenges faced by the different actors in the food system to be more easily identified. Because of the emphasis upon independencies, the systems approach encourages collaboration between interconnected actors and draws attention to critical leverage points in the system as a whole, where policies and interventions can not only be more coherently interfaced but be exponentially more effective (Meadows 1999).

The creation of shared policy 'spaces' enables a coming-together of diverse actors in the food system and facilitates communication and interaction leading to a more holistic understanding of the issues. Examples include initiatives such as AGree, A Shared Meal, The Arlie Conference, and the International Conference on Global Food Security, which was launched in 2013. Studies have also started to focus on tracing and mapping the interrelationships between food production, ecological sustainability and human health (see for example Ericksen 2008; Erickson, Ingram & Liverman 2009; Harvie 2006; Jackson et al. 2009; Kreuter et al. 2004; Lichtfouse et al. 2009; Muller et al. 2009; Wallinga 2009; Wallinga Schoonover & Muller 2009), as well as how quality and value are embedded in the food supply chain (Gereffi, Lee & Christian 2009; Noe & Alroe 2010).

The systems approach enables the development of frameworks to model the relationship between actors; the various issues and concerns of each; the range of policies and interventions and the social, cultural, economic, political, environmental and technological factors that affect the food system as a whole. For example, in an examination and synthesis of existing models of agriculture, food, nutrition, health and environmental systems, Sobal, Khan and Bisogni (1998) developed an integrated model of the food and nutrition system. This model comprised of three sub-systems (i.e., producer, consumer and nutrition) and nine stages (i.e., production, processing, distribution acquisition, preparation, consumption, digestion, transport, and metabolism). It also identified critical linkages between the different disciplines that deal with the food and nutrition system. Taking a social and natural science perspective (with particular emphasis on food systems, food security and social welfare), Ericksen (2008) synthesized the disparate literature on food systems, food security and global environmental change to develop an overarching framework for understanding the multiple components and interactions, key drivers and processes, impacts and feedback loops, societal outcomes and trade-offs in the food system.

In a similar vein, Neff and colleagues (2009) presented a conceptual model that illustrates how food system conditions affect the broad and local community food system. Their model draws attention to the interaction between meta- and micro- systems, and other aspects of the social environment, which in turn can explain different communities' diet and health disparities. Finally, Block and colleagues (2011) introduced the 'food well-being' (FWB) concept and advanced a framework for understanding the socio-cultural factors that govern people's attitudes and behaviours towards food. The FWB concept comprises five dimensions: food socialization, food literacy, food marketing, food availability, and food policy, each of which function on both individual and societal levels.

As can be seen, there is no lack of interest in or frameworks available for understanding the workings of the food system. Despite these advances however, regulators continue to operate within the confines of their respective silos/domains and attempt to manage the system as if it were a series of disparate problems occurring in isolation. Further, although there are many junctures within the food system for aligning and coordinating policies, initiatives and interventions (Muller et al. 2009), rarely do regulators capitalize on these opportunities.

We suspect that these regulatory errors occur for two reasons. First, there is a lack of a common, unified, agreed-upon goal that ties the various actors involved in the food system together. Although several scholars have advanced the notion that effective design of the food system requires equal consideration be given to environmental sustainability, economic and social goals (Harvie, Mikkelsen & Shak 2009; Story, Hamm, and Wallinga 2009a, 2009b), actors continue to impose their own goals and agendas onto others, hold fast to their own frameworks and preferred methods, debase the contribution of work taking place in other disciplines and suggest that one particular issue is the most pressing or more critical to the exclusion of others. For example, public health experts assert that the primary focus of food and agriculture policy should be on improving health and preventing obesity (Jackson et al. 2009; Lang 2009; Muller et al. 2009; Wallinga, Schoonover & Muller 2009). Whether done so purposefully or not (we assume that it is not), doing so has the effect of further alienating other actors and thwarting cooperative efforts and behaviours, and overshadowing other important goals.

Second, in terms of the regulatory literature and practice, there simply does not exist a theory and method for regulating such complex systems. The underlying assumption of each of the systems frameworks discussed above (and the systems approach in general) is the need for cohesion and coordination between the various actors in the food system. While the importance of coordination and cohesiveness between the actors is widely acknowledged, and the various issues and concerns of each, the range of policies, initiatives and interventions in place, as well as the social, cultural, economic, political, environmental and technological factors that affect the food system as a whole is known, the ways in which coordination and cohesiveness is to be achieved remains unknown. Put another way, there remains a notable absence of a coherent regulatory design for managing interrelatedness, coherently coordinating actors and dealing with the diversity of problems associated with the food system.

To this end, we introduce and discuss the theory underpinning our proposed regulatory framework: The Theory of Coherent Regulation. We then proceed to provide an overview of the steps that should be taken to develop a coherent regulatory design for the food system.

## The theory of coherent regulation and the food system

In the 1970s, a body of literature investigating the limitations of regulation and, in more extreme cases, its failure began to emerge (Breyer 1979; Stigler 1971). In an effort to better understand the many causes of ineffective regulation, its unintended consequences and situations where the cost of regulating outweighed its benefits, several studies examined the characteristics of ineffective regulation. In a seminal work, Breyer (1979) identified one main cause of regulatory failure as arising from the mismatch between the problem being addressed and the regulatory method chosen to solve the problem—a type of incoherence. Extending Breyer's early thinking, Sheehy and Feaver (2014), Feaver and Sheehy (2014) developed the Theory of Coherent Regulation (herein Coherence Theory)—a theory designed to address the common mistakes of regulatory design and offers an analytical framework that is not only capable of addressing complex problems at a systems level but is also flexible enough to encompass and address multiple problems simultaneously, thereby minimizing the risk of regulatory frictions, failure and unintended consequences.

Before describing the main characteristics of Coherence Theory, it is helpful to discuss three issues. First, what do we mean by the term 'regulation'? The term regulation is typically thought of as a rule made by an authority that has a mandatory compliance requirement (Smith 2002). Failure to comply has consequences (e.g., fines and penalties). Advances in regulatory theory take a broader view of regulation. More contemporary definitions of the term 'regulation' liken it to the term 'governance' and, more precisely, a method of governance. In this sense, regulation extends beyond the creation and imposition of rules. It is a governing framework that is comprised of different configurations of rules, drivers, powers, checks and balances, with compliance and enforcement mechanisms used to create, modify, prohibit or discipline human behaviours. Regulatory systems not only involve rule frameworks but are active systems that require management, usually by specialized organizational structures that are responsible for the administration, enforcement and application of a range of regulatory tools and techniques to oversee the behavioural change required to achieve a desired policy objective or outcome (Sheehy & Feaver 2014).

Second, there are many approaches, tools and techniques available for use by regulators to govern behaviour. In recent times, there has been a movement away from traditional command and control regulatory approaches, tools and techniques towards more flexible and even experimental forms of governance. It has become increasingly common to entrust private actors such as industry associations, NGOs, market participants and the media to promote behavioural change in a range of areas, ranging from corporate social responsibility to land use reform and climate change mitigation. However, an evaluation of these alternative forms of governance reveals that the use of contemporary approaches may not adequately address the problem at hand. For example, the personal accountability approach, with particular emphasis on consumer education, appears to be a popular tool for addressing issues pertaining to public health. Analysis suggests that this approach has not been particularly effective in changing behaviour (Harris et al. 2009). Further, in an examination of the distributive outcomes of private governance tools, such as quality assurance schemes, certification and labelling programs for addressing global sustainability concerns, Kalfagianni (2013) found that under these private initiatives, rule-setters tend to benefit more than rule-takers and rule-users. This raises the following question: On what basis should decisions regarding the appropriateness of tools and techniques be made? In the next section, we demonstrate how

Coherence Theory can be used to guide the selection of regulatory approaches, tools and techniques (and combinations thereof) for managing the problem at hand—the food system.

Third, consistency and harmony within and among different aspects, processes and components of the governing framework (i.e., coherence) is critical to the success or failure of any regulatory system (Breyer 1979; Feaver & Sheehy 2014; Sheehy & Feaver 2014). Each aspect, process and component of a regulatory system must logically connect to other components in such a way that each complements, or at the very least does not adversely affect, other aspects of the system. As is evident from a review of the literature, the existing regulatory framework governing the food system is ineffective—for the most part because there is a lack of coherence in its design. By applying Coherence Theory, we demonstrate how coherence can be built in and sustained throughout the regulatory system.

The application Coherence Theory begins by appreciating that regulation has two dimensions: a normative dimensions and a positive dimension (Sheehy and Feaver 2013). The normative dimension deals with abstract policy considerations that underpin the design of a regulatory framework. It represents the initial, normative blueprint which informs the formulation of regulatory objectives, the framing of policies and the choice of the most appropriate regulatory tools. The positive dimension takes the normative blueprint and translates these policy choices into the legal architecture of a regulatory system.

The normative and positive dimensions themselves each consist of various components. Each component represents a set of processes and decisions. The main components of the normative dimension can be summarized as: (1) defining the organizing problem; (2) characterising the organizing problem; (3) framing the organizing problem; and (4) selecting the regulatory approach. The choices made in relation to these four components inform the composition of the components that comprise the positive dimension and ultimately make up the legal architecture of a regulatory system. Decisions pertaining to the legal architecture take place on three levels: (1) structural; (2) substantive; and (3) operational. While ideally, regulatory design should take place as a step-by-step process, in practice these steps do not proceed in a linear fashion. For the purpose of theoretical exposition, however, the application of the Coherence Theory to the food system will be discussed one step (i.e., component) at a time.

In applying coherence theory to the wicked problem of regulating the food system, as mentioned in the Introduction, the focus of the analysis below is necessarily broad. Rather than examining discrete problems in their issue 'silos' or 'domains', which we believe is misleading if not detrimental, the analysis will examine the broader coordination challenges that have been neglected by most food system policy studies. It is important to understand that at this broad level of application we are dealing with 'meta-policy'—the development of overarching plans that provide a means of better coordinating and integrating the innumerable more specific and technical policy and regulatory arrangements that fall within its umbrella. The purpose of fashioning a clear meta-policy is to provide a blueprint with which to better coordinate, harmonize and integrate the more discrete policy and regulatory initiatives that fall within its scope.

## Defining the organizing problem.

More often than not, regulatory solutions (i.e., policies, initiatives and interventions) are developed without taking the first step of clearly defining and understanding the nature of the problem to be resolved. As a result, regulatory stakeholders may not be discussing and developing solutions to solve the same problem. In the first instance, there must be some agreement that there is a problem that requires regulatory attention. Second, there needs to be agreement about what the problem is. For example, the food system encompasses problems such as food scarcity, food quality, environmental degradation of food producing soils, market failures and economic opportunities, just to name a few. Given the complexity of the food system, attention must be given to how a wide variety of inter-connected systems—social, environmental and economic systems—fit together, and are affected by behavioural adjustments at the various stages of the supply-chain. Because the problems affecting the food system as a whole can involve one, both, or all three of these supporting systems, up to seven permutations and hence, seven distinct categories of problems can be identified (see Figure 4.1 below).

**Figure 4.1 – Defining the organizing problem**

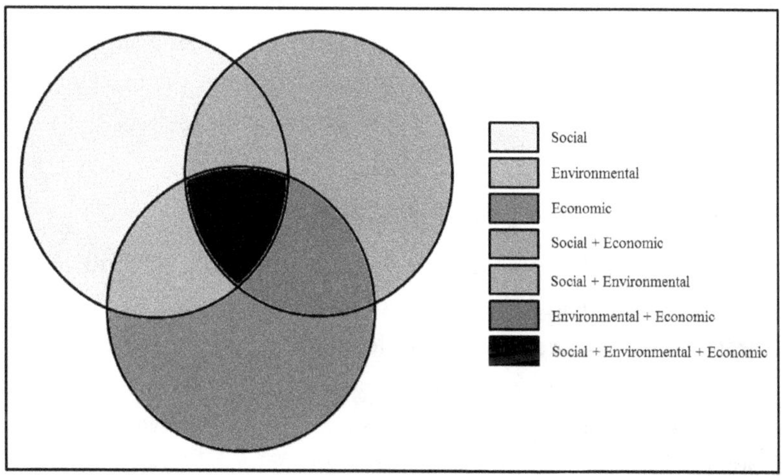


Categorizing problems affecting the food system in terms of either pure social, environmental and economic problems, a combination of

two, or all three, illustrates the point that problems impacting on the food system are interrelated. Graphically categorizing the range of food system problems as illustrated in Figure 1 helps to identify where and on what issues they overlap. Where overlap occurs, multiple interconnected problems can be grouped and approached holistically as a 'problem space'.

Importantly, taking a step back from the immediate problem facilitates consideration of the complexities of the larger food system and allows a common meta-goal to emerge: a food system that makes available, accessible, and affordable healthy food to meet current food needs while maintaining healthy ecosystems (i.e., minimal negative impact on the environment) that provides food for generations to come, encourages local production and distribution infrastructures, and that is human and just (i.e., protecting farmers and other workers, consumers and communities) (Storey, Hamm & Wallinga 2009a, 2009b). The identification and articulation of common problem spaces is the first step towards defining the organizing problem and developing a meta-policy blueprint that coordinates the more discrete regulatory interventions at more specific levels of analysis.

## Characterizing the organizing problem

Once an organizing problem or problem space has been identified, the second step in designing a coherent regulatory framework involves characterizing the organizing problem. An organizing problem need not be viewed through a single lens—a problem can be viewed through multiple lenses simultaneously and no single perspective need be the correct one. The old saying that 'one person's trash is another person's treasure' illustrates this assertion.

The characterization process does, however, involve classifying the organizing problem as having the attributes that can be described as being: a social issue, a risk or an opportunity. Social issues can be generalized as a problem that affects the whole of society and its stability or advancement. Social issues that threaten or harm social stability are referred to as systemic harms. Systemic harms, not unlike public goods, often require public attention largely because fashioning an effective response to these types of problems requires a high degree of organization and coordination—hence, their classification as social coordination problems. Referring to such systemic threats, social coordination problems can be described as arising when "organized society appears to be seriously threatened by an inability to order relationships among people" (Ainsworth 1972: 141; see also Raab & Selznick 1964).

Society's inability to spontaneously order relationships to effectively deal with such a threat or to facilitate seizing a chance to advance the public good leads to the proposition that social coordination problems must be addressed by another means—usually a public authority, such as a government. These means are usually centralised and capable of marshalling resources and putting institutional arrangements in place to contain, minimize, mitigate or eliminate the systemic threat or harm. For example, the public health issues surrounding food production and consumption require organized and coordinated oversight mechanisms such as public health and safety inspections to ensure that the food meets national standards of quality and fitness.

Unlike social coordination problems, the second characterisation of organising problems is as a risk. Risks do not have ubiquitous systemic effects. Risks are defined in the large literature as "the probability that a particular adverse event will occur during a stated period of time, or result from a particular challenge" (Baldwin & Cave 1999: 13). That is to say, risks are both temporally and spatially bound.

Furthermore, risks have a number of additional characteristics not found in social problems. For example, risks may be either voluntarily undertaken or involuntariliy imposed, individually or collectively borne, naturally occurring or the result of social arrangements and practices (Lee 1981; Swedlow et al. 2009).

Further, unlike social coordination problems that are universal in nature, the temporal and spatial characteristics of risks means that a more limited class of actors—particularly at the level of the individual—are more likely to be associated with the organizing problem. Most importantly, if the aggregation of these individual risks generates social costs, research indicates that those social costs can be mitigated more optimally through some form of collective action response. As such, risks can be characterized as collective action problems where "rational individual action can lead to a strictly Pareto-inferior outcome, that is, an outcome which is strictly less preferred by every individual than at least one other outcome" (Taylor 1987: 56). In order to avoid a Pareto-inferior outcome, a regulatory response in the form of a collective action solution is a more optimal way of "provid[ing] mutual protection against risk" (Ostrom 2000: 138).

The line between social coordination problems (social issues) and collective action problems (risks) is at times a blurry one. For example, the need for food standards can be characterized as both a social issue and alleviating a risk. As a social issue, food standards protect the public good of general health and well-being. The primary target of such social protection regulation is the general public. Accordingly, a universal, coordinated solution is required to meet that objective. Alternatively, food safety can also be viewed as a risk. Food producers and processors must meet health and safety standards at a much more localized level—the farm or the plant—to avoid specific risks, such as contamination. Accordingly, regulations targeted at producer behaviour and applied on a site by site basis may take on a very different character to broader public good regulation of social issues.

Finally, regulation may be imposed to provide an opportunity. This form of regulation can be viewed as an enabler where a public authority grants some form of right or license to a particular actor, such as the grant of a gene or drug patent. Opportunity or enabling regulation can also be viewed in different ways. For example, a risk of starvation is simultaneously an economic opportunity for a person selling food. It is not that one or the other is the only correct characterization—an organizing problem can be characterized as any one or a combination of the three (See Figure 4.2 below).

**Figure 4.2 – Characterizing the organizing problem**

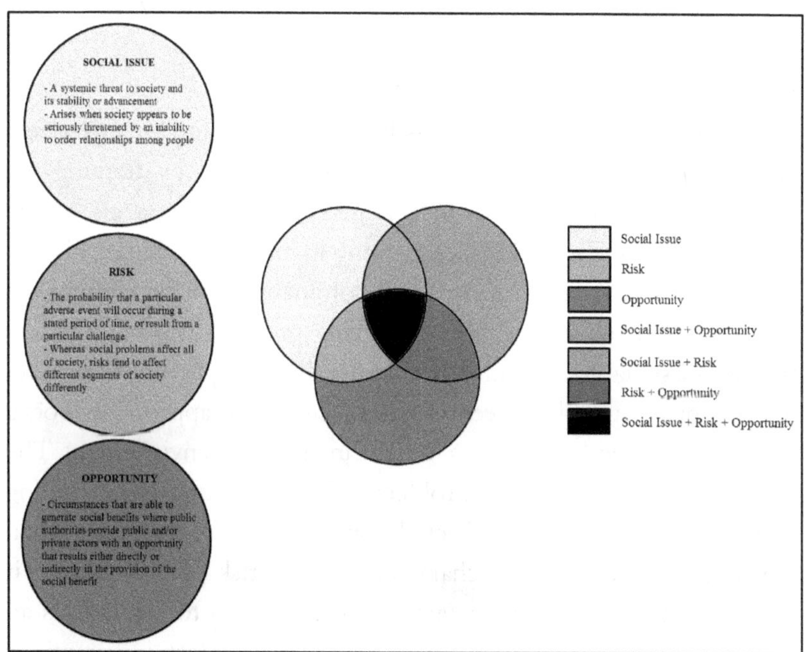

Fashioning a meta-policy, such as a national food strategy, has the character of a social coordination problem. The objective of such a policy, as mentioned above, is to provide a framework that enables more discrete regulatory problems to be coherently brought into the scope of the umbrella policy. That is not to say that more particular risks and opportunities do not have an important place within the framework. It is important however, to note that risk- and opportunity- based regulatory interventions are targeted to narrower groups of actors engaged in specific activities but still under the broader umbrella. Accordingly, the development of coherent meta-policy requires a form of normative ordering of issues and their policies within the regulatory spaces being coordinated. This more abstract exercise takes on a more tangible form when the normative ordering is translated and framed as policy, discussed below.

### Framing the organizing problem

Once the organizing problem has been identified and characterized, policy makers next have to formalize it as policy by framing the parameters of the problem in a manner that corresponds to the problem's social context. Policy framing involves two things. First, it requires a choice be made regarding a dominant characterization—the determination of whether the organizing problem will be primarily treated as a social coordination problem, a risk or opportunity? Second, the organizing problem needs to be placed in an appropriate social context, in essence, connecting it to the institutional environment. The way in which the organizing problem is framed is critical to garnering 'buy-in' from the various affected constituents. For example, when the organizing problem is characterized as a risk of soil salinity, it is less helpful to frame it as careless farming than to frame it as an opportunity to develop innovative ways to improve farming practices.

The importance of framing goes beyond the political-social implications of policy-making. Framing is equally important in the development of regulation because it is forms the lens used to fashion black letter solutions. For example, framing the organizing problem as an economic/market-driven opportunity leads politicians to seek market-based regulatory solutions that shift primary responsibility to private actors. Alternatively, framing the organizing problem as a broader social problem will lead policy-makers to choose regulatory interventions that seek to organize and position actors within an institutional landscape in order to ensure that their interactions achieve broader societal goals by generating social benefits that are of a more systemic nature. Selecting a specific framing does not involve choosing one framing over another. Rather it requires better coordinating regulatory initiatives and placing them within more coherent arrangement of policies and interventions. Although this might be seen as a direct challenge to neo-liberal market-based approaches, it is thoroughly consistent with one of the primary assumptions, namely, that markets can be used in areas where governments have traditionally produced and/or delivered goods and services. More particularly, the proposed view is consistent with new models of governance that seek to re-define the role of government as a director and coordinator rather than 'intervener'. Governance is required where higher orders of coordination are required whereas market solutions can be used to solve individual needs and distributing individualised opportunities. Effective solutions to social problems, however, require positioning actors, institutions within a broad framework to enable market mechanisms to operate more effectively within their appropriate policy space.

## Selecting the regulatory approach

Any policy which does not set out a coherent plan for achieving its objectives is deficient. Additionally, once objectives are defined, they must be aligned coherently to the means or methods selected to achieve those objectives. The framing exercise focuses more on the objective setting part of the equation which leads to the methods selected. When the organizing problem is framed as a long-term environmental sustainability issue, a coherent regulatory approach will be one that does not favour short-term profit making, as is common to market-based approaches. Likewise, when the organizing problem is framed as a public health issue, the regulatory approach cannot be focused on individual choice. Instead, it takes on the character of a broader public problem and hence its solution is properly viewed as a public good.

With new regulatory technologies comes a wider choice of regulatory devices that extend beyond the traditional command-and-control approaches available to policy makers. These include regulatory devices ranging from information and disclosure regimes (commonly advocated in the food industry through labelling) and tax incentives and disincentives (such as increased taxes on unhealthy foods or tax deductions on gymnasium memberships and similar devices) suited to individual framings, through to organisation or enterprise focused framings, which may also use disclosure and tax incentives and disincentives (such as increased taxes for production of unhealthy foods or tax deductions for improved nutritional quality), and industry wide devices such as voluntary measures like the global multinational corporations' agreement concerning the use of palm oil from sustainable plantations.

In developing a systemic approach to food system regulation, it is imperative on policy makers to consider the full range of regulatory techniques available to address the problems of the food system. This imperative rejects relying on a dominant approach, such as markets for ideological reasons, as has been the case with recent regulatory design trends. Different aspects of complex problems can only be dealt with using different and more appropriate regulatory tools. While a meta-policy such as a national or transnational food strategy is clearly coordinative and directive in nature, the sub-policies and regulatory interventions that fit under its umbrella must be fashioned using the approaches that are most suitable for their problem space. For example, some public health initiatives may be adequately served using information and education as the most effective approach where the problems can readily be dealt with in that manner and the affected populations are susceptible to changing behaviour on the basis of information and education. Economic problems affecting production and distribution may be more appropriately using market solutions rather than centralized interventions such as buying pools, marketing boards and subsidies. One thing that history has taught us is that regulation will inevitably fail if the wrong approach is selected to address ill-defined policy objectives.

## Fashioning the legal architecture

Once the normative issues have been determined and general policy objective settled, it must be translated into a formal policy statement and usually, a statutory regulatory scheme. The core issue in designing an effective regulatory system is positioning and connecting key actors. Regulation, like any other social configuration, is a networked relationship of actors who are either required or expected to behave in particular ways. Traditionally, most regulation has been designed using model of hierarchical structure where power emanates from a government and is delegated to regulatory actors that command

and control even lower power actors. In recent years, a significant change in thinking as to how regulation is structured has occurred affecting the allocation and distribution of power and authority within regulatory systems. In brief, this has meant investigating and experimenting with structures in which greater responsibility for regulating has been shifted to regulatees themselves (Havinga, Fuchs & Kalfagianni 2011).

Food regulation is an example of an area in which governments have been willing to try experimental regulatory approaches and their corresponding structural innovations. Governments have adopted an industry promoted framing and approach, which advocated the shift of significant portion of the cost of and responsibility for regulating the food system to industry actors in the form of principles-based self-regulatory arrangements. This approach has simultaneously required a partial withdrawal from the regulatory enterprise by governments who have shifted their participation in the experiment to that of an oversight actor rather than a participatory and interventionist actor engaged in regulatory roles. This stepping back by the public authorities in the food as well as other areas has led to wide variety of defective and even failed regulatory systems. These failures can be seen across areas ranging from research and development failures in the pharmaceutical and chemical industries, to increased safety violations and animal cruelty in abattoirs and the live export trade to failures to protect natural water resources in terms of safe water for populations, allocations for nature preservation and irrigation.

The structure and configuration of the administrative machinery that is part of a regulatory system is also critical to its success. Administration itself does not occur spontaneously and nor is it cost-free. Effective administration requires appropriate design and resourcing. For example, administrators of consumer food regulation require resources to deal with consumer groups, whereas regulators administering technical standards for food producers require expertise in food production as well as regulatory administration. Moreover, resourcing and coordination of effective oversight mechanisms is required in order to both induce compliance as well as to monitor whether regulatory objectives are being met. Some aspects of the food system require rigorous oversight. Other aspects of the food system can function efficiently with less stringent oversight. The challenge in designing the legal architecture of a regulatory system is determining the most effective and efficient structures.

A logical function of a regulator charged with the responsibility of overseeing the implementation of a national food strategy whose main objective is coordinative, is to ensure that the regulatory regimes that fall under its umbrella are designed using appropriate approaches and legal structures, that administrative arrangements are appropriate and that powers and functions are appropriately identified and distributed. Much regulation fails where the approaches and structures do not coincide or are somehow mismatched. As such, a national food system regulator would be expected to play the role of a coordinator not only by ensuring that sub-schemes fit within the overall food system strategy better, but a national regulator would need the power to direct appropriate reform to better target and position specialist regulation.

## Determining substantive rights and duties

Every regulatory system has substantive rights and duties, meaning, who will be allowed to do what, on what basis, and how those things will be done. These are all matter of law and form the substantive aspects of regulatory systems. Determining the substantive rights and duties of the various actors within the food system follows from the five steps, as discussed above.

In the context of food system regulation, substantive duties could include farming with obligations to protect the environment. Such substantive duties already exist in many areas of farm production—from soil erosion control to tax incentives for maintaining wood lots and restrictions on the use of pharmaceuticals in livestock production. Similar substantive duties are present throughout the food system. However, they are incoherent, often poorly considered, misguided and inappropriately applied. Coherent food regulation requires consideration of substantive obligations not independently, as they usually are, but as part of a coherent regulatory system addressing the organizing problem.

## Operating the regulatory system

The operation of a regulatory system requires careful attention. This last aspect of coherent regulatory design is to do with testing for compliance and providing enforcement (or reinforcement where positive incentives are provided), in the appropriate situation. Each part of the regulatory system needs to have its operations well considered, its staff trained, and well resourced.

## Conclusion

Designing a coherent regulatory framework for the food system is certainly a challenge. It cannot be done locally, or in isolation geographically, or within the system. By applying the Theory of Coherent Regulation, we demonstrate how coherence can be built in and sustained throughout the regulatory system—from problem identification to the design of policies, initiatives and interventions and selection of regulatory approaches, tools and techniques, through to the design of the legal architecture for implementing and evaluating the regulatory framework. The resultant regulatory framework is not overburdened with ideology. Rather, it is a pragmatic approach. It is apolitical in the sense that it does not privilege the goals and agendas of any one actor over another. It combines aspects of public and private regulatory tools to allow for an effective balance between the competing interests of different actors, as well the coordination of the multiple constituents of the food system. Perhaps most importantly, this approach allows for a more effective way to address the great issues facing the human population today as well as tomorrow: a world today in which half of the population suffers malnutrition while the other half struggles with obesity, and a world tomorrow which anticipates a doubling of the population by 2050.

Developing this systems approach into the future requires more than research into the successes and failures of existing regulatory approaches to the food system, although that would certainly be informative. Developing a coherent approach to food regulation requires significant research into the nature of the problem, the challenges and limitations of current approaches and solutions to these problems and directions. A simple focus on individual choices and expanding the reach of markets is a prescription for disaster for a problem too complex to be left to the frailties of individual human decision making capacities. The challenges of feeding healthy food to a burgeoning global population are too complex and too important to be left to the random orderings of markets. Effective solutions to these problems require the hand of publicly motivated coherent governance.

## References


Ainsworth, CH 1972, *Selected Readings for Introductory Sociology*, MSS Information Corporation, New York.

Baldwin, R & Cave, M 1999, *Understanding Regulation: Theory, Strategy, and Practice*, Oxford University Press, Oxford.

Block, LG, Grier, SA, Childers, TL, Davis, B, Ebert, JEJ, Kumanyika, S, Laczniak, RN, Machin, JE, Motley, CM, Peracchio, L, Pettigrew, S, Scott, M & van Ginkel, BMNG 2011, 'From nutrients to nurturance: A conceptual introduction to food well-being', *Journal of Public Policy & Marketing*, vol. 30, no. 1, pp. 5-13.

Bonanno, A & Constance, DH 2001, 'Corporate strategies in the global era: The case of mega-hog farms in the Texas Panhandle Region', *International Journal of Sociology of Agriculture and Food*, vol. 9, no. 1, pp. 5-28.

Breyer, S 1979, 'Analysing regulatory failure: Mismatches, less restrictive alternatives, and reform', *Harvard Law Review*, vol. 92, no. 3, pp. 547-609.

Brownson, RC, Fielding, JE & Maylahn, CM 2009, 'Evidence-based public health: A fundamental concept for public health practice', *Annual Review of Public Health*, vol. 30, pp. 175-201.

Ericksen, PJ 2008, 'Conceptualizing food systems for global environmental change', *Global Environmental Change*, vol. 18, pp. 234-245.

Ericksen, PJ, Ingram, JSI & Liverman DM 2009, 'Food security and global environmental change: Emerging challenges', *Environmental Science and Policy*, vol. 12, pp. 373-377.

Feaver, D & Sheehy, B 2014, 'A positive theory of coherent regulation'

Finkelstein, E, French, S, Variyam, JN & Haines PS 2004, 'Pros and cons of proposed interventions to promote healthy eating', *American Journal of Preventative Medicine*, vol. 27, no. 3S, pp. 163-171.

Foster, C, Green, K, Bleda, M, Dewick, P, Evans, B, Flynn A & Mylan, J 2006, *Environmental impacts of food production and consumption: A report to the Department for Environment, Food and Rural Affairs*, viewed 17 August 2013, <http://www.ifr.ac.uk/waste/Reports/DEFRA-Environmental%20Impacts%20of%20Food%20Production%20%20Consumption.pdf>

Fuchs, D, Kalfagianni, A & Havinga T 2011, 'Actors in private food governance: The legitimacy of retail standards and multistakeholder initiatives with civil society participation', *Agriculture and Human Values*, vol. 28, no. 3, pp. 353-367.

Gereffi, G, Lee, J & Christian M 2009, 'US-based food and agricultural value chains and their relevance to health diets', *Journal of Hunger and Environmental Nutrition*, vol. 4, no. 3-4, pp. 357-374.

Hamm, MW 2009, 'Principles for framing a healthy food system', *Journal of Hunger and Environmental Nutrition*, vol. 4, pp. 241-250.

Harris, JL, Pomeranz, JL, Lobstein T & Bronell KD 2009, 'A crisis in the marketplace: How food marketing contributes to childhood obesity and what can be done', *Annual Review of Public Health*, vol. 30, pp. 211-225.

Harvie, J 2006, *Redefining healthy food: An ecological health approach to food production, distribution and procurement*, Centre for Health Design and Health Care Without Harm, viewed 17 August 2013, < http://noharm.org/lib/downloads/food/Redefining_Healthy_Food.pdf>

Harvie, J, Mikkelsen, L & Shak L 2009, 'A new health care prevention agenda: Sustainable food procurement and agriculture policy', *Journal of Hunger and Environmental Nutrition*, vol. 4, no. 3-4, pp. 409-429.

Jackson, RJ, Minjares, R, Naumoff, KS, Shrimali, BP & Martin, LK 2009, 'Agriculture policy is health policy', *Journal of Hunger and Environmental Nutrition*, vol. 4, no. 3-4, pp. 393-408.

Kaditi, EA 2013, 'Market dynamics in food supply chains: The impact of globalization and consolidation on firms' market power', *Agribusiness*, vol. 29, no. 4, pp. 410-425.

Kalfagianni, A 2013, 'Addressing the global sustainability challenge: The potential and pitfalls of private governance from the perspective of human capabilities', *Journal of Business Ethics*, pp.1-14.

Kreuter, MW, De Rosa, C, Howze, EH & Baldwin GT 2004, 'Understanding wicked problems: A key to advancing environmental health promotion', *Health Education and Behaviour*, vol. 31, no.(4), pp. 441-454.

Lang, T 2009, 'Reshaping the food system for ecological public health', *Journal of Hunger and Environmental Nutrition*, vol. 4, no. 3-4, pp. 315-335.

Lee, TR 1981, 'The public's perception of risk and the question of irrationality', *Proceedings of the Royal Society of London, Series A: Mathematical and Physical Sciences*, vol. 376, no. 1764, pp. 5-16.

Lichtfouse, E, Navarrete, M, Debaeke, P, Souchere, V, Alberola, C & Menassieu, J 2009, 'Agronomy for sustainable agriculture: A review', *Agronomy for Sustainable Development*, vol. 29, pp. 1-6.

Malhi, L, Karanfil, O, Merth, T, Acheson, M, Palmer, A & Finegood, DT 2009, 'Places to intervene to make complex food systems more health, green, fair and affordable', *Journal of Hunger and Environmental Nutrition*, vol. 4, no. 3-4, pp. 466-476.

Meadows, D 1999, *Leverage points: Places to intervene in a system*, Sustainability Institute: 1-19. viewed 17 August 2013, <www.sustainabilityinstitute.org/pubs/Leverage_Points.pdf>

Muller, M, Tagtow, A, Roberts, SL & Macdougall, E 2009, 'Aligning food systems policies to advance public health', *Journal of Hunger and Environmental Nutrition*, vol. 4, no. 3-4, pp. 225-240.

Neff, RA, Palmer, AM, McKenzie, SE & Lawrence, RS 2009, 'Food systems and public health disparities', *Journal of Hunger and Environmental Nutrition*, vol. 4, no. 3-4, pp. 282-314.

Noe, E & Alroe HF 2010, 'Quality, coherence and co-operation: A framework for studying the mediation qualities in food networks and collective marketing strategies', *International Journal of Sociology of Agriculture and Food*, vol. 18, no. 1, pp. 12-27.

Ostrom, E 2000, 'Collective action and the evolution of social norms', *The Journal of Economic Perspectives*, vol. 14, no. 3, pp. 167-158.

Pratt, MG, Macera, CA, Sallis, JF, O'Donnell, M & Frank, LD 2004, 'Economic interventions to promote physical activity: Application of the SLOTH Model', *American Journal of Preventative Medicine*, vol. 27, no. 3S, pp. 136-145.

Raab, E & Selznick, GJ 1964, *Major Social Problems*, Harper & Row, Michigan.

Rittel, HWJ & Webber, MM 1973, 'Dilemmas in a general theory of planning', *Policy Sciences*, vol. 4, no. 2, pp. 155-169.

Scammon, DL, Keller, PA, Albinsson, PA, Bahl, S, Catlin, JR, Haws, KL, Kees, J, King, T, Miller, EG, Mirabito, AM, Peter, PC & Schindler, RM 2011,

'Transforming consumer health', *Journal of Public Policy and Marketing*, vol. 30, no. 1, pp. 14-22.

Sheehy, B & Feaver, D 2014, 'A normative theory of coherent regulation'.

Shill, J, Mavoa, H, Allender, S, Lawrence, M, Sacks, G, Peeters, A, Crammond, B & Swinburn, B 2011, 'Government regulation to promote healthy food environments: A review from inside state governments', *Obesity Reviews*, vol. 13, pp. 162-173.

Smith, DK 2002, 'What is regulation: A reply to Julia Black', *Australian Journal of Legal Philosophy*, vol. 37, pp. 1-46.

Sobal, J, Khan, LK, & Bisogni, C 1998, 'A conceptual model of the food and nutrition system', *Social Science and Medicine*, vol. 47, no. 7, pp. 853-863.

Stigler, GJ 1971, 'The theory of economic regulation', *The Bell Journal of Economics and Management Science*, vol. 2, no. 1, pp. 3-21.

Story, M, Hamm, MW & Wallinga D 2009a, 'Food systems and public health: Linkages to achieve healthier diets and healthier communities', *Journal of Hunger and Environmental Nutrition*, vol. 4, no. 3-4, pp. 219-224.

Story, M, Hamm, MW & Wallinga D 2009b, 'Research and action priorities for linking public health, food systems and sustainable agriculture: Recommendations from the Arlie Conference', *Journal of Hunger and Environmental Nutrition*, vol. 4, no. 3-4, pp. 477-485.

Swedlow, B, Kall, D, Zhou, Z, Hammitt, JK & Wiener, JB 2009, 'Theorizing and Generalizing about Risk Assessment and Regulation through Comparative Nested Analysis of Representative Cases', *Law & Policy*, vol. 31, no. 2, pp. 236-269.

Taylor, M 1987, *The Possibility of Cooperation*, Cambridge University Press, Essex.

Trochim, WM, Cabrera, DA, Milstein, B, Gallagher, RS & Leischow, SJ 1996, 'Practical challenges of systems thinking and modelling in public health', *American Journal of Public Health*, vol. 96, no. 3, pp. 538-546.

Viola, D, Arno, PS, Maroko, AR, Schechter, CB, Sohler, N, Rundle, A, Neckerman, KM & Maantay, J 2013, 'Overweight and obesity: Can we reconcile evidence about supermarkets and fast food retailers for public health policy?', *Journal of Public Health Policy*, vol. 34, no. 3, pp. 424-438.

Wallinga, D 2009, 'Today's food system: How healthy is it?', *Journal of Hunger and Environmental Nutrition*, vol. 4, no. 3-4, pp. 251-281.

Wallinga, D, Schoonover, H & Muller, M 2009, 'Considering the contribution of US agricultural policy to the obesity epidemic: Overview and opportunities', *Journal of Hunger and Environmental Nutrition*, vol. 4, no. 1, 3-19.

# 5

# Exporting packaged foods to China: The product customisation imperative

Nicholas Grigoriou

## Introduction: China's economic miracle

China is one of the more rapidly developing countries in the world. In the last thirty years, the annual growth rate of China's gross domestic product was more than eight per cent, the highest rate in recent world history (World Bank 2011). During this period, China experienced the same degree of industrialisation that took two centuries to occur in Europe (Summers 2007). To some extent, the prospect of the global economy is critically dependent on the rate of economic growth in China (Sridhar and Wan 2010).

China's economic growth has brought increasing prosperity to Chinese households, lifting tens of millions out of poverty at unprecedented rates. Large growth rates in real per capita income are also observed in urban and rural household surveys: seven per cent per annum since 1978 for urban households and five per cent per annum since 1985 for rural households (Chamon and Filho 2014). So impressive is China's economic transformation, that the nation managed to lower the proportion of the population living in poverty from 20 per cent to fewer than 10 per cent during the 1980s (Datt 1999).

China is currently the most active internationalising economy among the developing nations. Investment from both domestic and international sources has been increasing over the years (Chadee, Qiu, and Rose 2003). China is the second largest recipient of foreign direct investment in the world with more than 330,000 foreign investment projects operating in the country in 2007 (Luo 2007). Much of this investment centres on 14 special economic zones formed in 1984 (Wei and Leung 2005). Moreover, rapid commercialisation of consumption did more than simply increase consumer choice and raises the material standard of living. It also broke the monopolies that had previously cast urban consumers in the role of supplicants to the state (Davis 2000).

One key element in Chinese liberalisation policies has been the promotion of consumption (Jussaume 2001; Li et al. 2009). Consumption among China's consumers is now being viewed by the Chinese political leadership as beneficial for a variety of reasons. These include:

- Improved well-being for general populace;
- The strengthening of demand as an element in promoting further growth; and
- The appeasement of citizens.

China is the largest producer and consumer of food in the world. Since the early 1980s, the agricultural food industry has undergone phenomenal expansion throughout the food supply chain, from agricultural production to trade, agricultural food processing to retailing, and from food service to advertising (Hawkes 2008). Armed with increasing disposable income from economic reforms and developing tastes, Chinese consumers are having their say in shaping the directions of this huge and growing market (Zhou et al. 2010). One manifestation of increased economic prosperity and increased personal income is that Chinese consumers are eating more meals away from the family home (Bai et al. 2010). Typically, these meals are consumed in take away outlets, canteens, and restaurants. Another manifestation of China's economic reforms is that foreign trade has played an increasing role in the national economy since reforms began in 1978 (Huang, Li and Rozelle 2003). These economic reforms have made it possible for food exporters to target China with their products. A key managerial decision in light of this export trade opportunity is the degree to which food products exported to China are customised or exported and sold as standardised products that closely resemble the product sold in the export marketer's home market.

## Food consumption in China

The consumption of food has often been analysed from the perspective that food choices are dictated by societal expectations (Escalas and Bettman 2003). From a specific China perspective, Denton and Kaixun (1995: 60) posit:

> Food consumption is influenced by historical, medical, social and cosmological factors. Food is also a primary component of Chinese festivals. In combination, these independent considerations produce a complex system of food preference and consumption that is unlike any experienced in the West.

Taking Denton and Kaixuan's comment into consideration, packaged food export decision makers must consider food preference and consumption patterns as an important variable in determining whether or not exported packaged foods to China require customisation, in what ways, and to what extent. Given the central importance of food in Chinese culture (Veeck and Burns 2005) and the historic vulnerability of the Chinese population to food insecurity (Gale and Huang 2007), export food product customisation decisions become a key managerial decision for food exporters targeting mainland China. With an abundance of new consumption options and increased spending in an era of economic reform, Chinese consumers have begun indulging in hedonic consumption in many consumer goods categories (Landwehr, et al. 2012).

A major issue facing China's government is to provide enough food for its ever expanding population, either through increased domestic product or imports (Roth, et al., 2008). The geographic and demographic distribution of China's population suggests varying nutritional needs. Cities such as Beijing, Shanghai and Guangzhou are some of the largest in the world, yet approximately 80 per cent of China's population lives in rural areas. Whilst the majority of China's food consumption is produced domestically, there is a growing importance on food importing. This has paved the way for packaged food exporters to consider China as an export destination.

### An overview of product customisation or product standardization

International marketing strategies may be differentiated according to the degree of customisation (or adaptation) versus standardisation pursued with respect to one or more marketing mix elements. A standardisation strategy involves uniform marketing mix elements across different national markets, whilst a customisation strategy involves the tailoring of marketing mix elements to each international market (Siraliova and Angelis 2006). Within a packaged food context, customisation refers, but is not limited to, the customisation of the product's packaging, ingredients, and labeling (Regmi and Gehlhar 2005).

## The argument for product standardisation

Proponents of product standardisation essentially argue that world markets have become more homogeneous and that a standardised approach to international product planning can generate advantages through economies of scale and greater efficiencies (Kogut 1985; Levitt 1983). Rapid advances in transportation and communication technologies have facilitated this trend towards homogenisation of world markets (Ohmae 1985). In light of this, Buatsi (1986) suggested that product standardisation can lower inventory handling, spare parts, and maintenance costs and the cost of training service personnel, although this argument appears less immediately compelling in the case of packaged food products, than in, consumer durables for example. Further, Levitt (1983) argues that well managed companies have moved from an emphasis on customising items to offering globally standardised products that are advanced, functional, reliable and low priced. He states that there are essentially two types of firms engaged in international marketing. The global corporation that "operates with resolute constancy, at low relative cost, as if the entire world (or major regions of it) were a single entity; it sells the same things the same way everywhere". The multinational corporation on the other hand, "adjusts its products and practices in each country, at high relative cost". Whilst Levitt does not dispute that countries have different national tastes, cultural preferences and business institutions, he believes these are 'vestiges of the past.' In a food context, Levitt cites generic examples of pita bread and pizza, being enjoyed everywhere in the world. These products target market segments that exist in worldwide proportions. He argues that rather than contradicting global homogenisation, they confirm it. Levitt also argues against the assumption that an extant difference must remain in place:

> I do not advocate the systematic disregard of local and nation differences. But a company's sensitivity to such differences does not require that it ignore the possibility of doing things differently or better (1983: 93).

Advocates of the product standardisation approach argue that in light of the accelerating internationalisation of world economies and the parallel increase in competition on a global scale, due to factors such as technological advancements, trade liberalization and economic integration, success lies in the development of universal marketing mix strategies (Leonidou 1996). Yet, while standardisation can offer economies of scale, it can also lead to suboptimal sales when it is inconsistent with the environment in the host market (Yip 2003). Schuh (2000) found that strong corporate cultures and management practices with regard to quality, innovation, and product performance are also antecedents of product standardisation. In light of this, managerial decision making regarding the product standardisation or customisation decision is an important factor for any organization seeking to market their food and beverage products into international markets.

## The argument for product customisation

Proponents of customised products for world markets cite the marketing concept as a guiding paradigm for export product development. The aim of the 'marketing concept' is to identify consumers with a given need and then provide them with an offering that satisfies that need in a manner superior to that of your competition (Kotler and Keller 2012), then the product offering (in this case a tangible food and beverage product) is critical. Empirical studies have tended to support the idea that marketers can meet consumers' needs over time better than the competition by offering a high variety product line (Kahn 1998). Boddewyn, Soehl, and Picard (1986) report that organisations perceive competition is the most important obstacle in standardising any element of the marketing. In light of this, Cavusgil, Zou and Naidu (1993) found that the most important consideration in a packaging and labelling customisation decision is the intensity of competition in the foreign market.

Given the importance product development plays in organisational success, Kotler (1986) asserts that international product failures have been caused by a lack of product customisation. Kotler advocates product customisation because consumer demand in different nations for specific product features is different, whilst Valenzuela and Dhar (2004) argue that product customisation allows decomposition of the purchase decision into a series of smaller sub problems affecting consumers' choice evaluation. Bardakci and Whitelock (2003) argue that customers now seek exactly what they need, when they need it and how they need it at affordable prices. They are not willing to wait for customised products, but are seeking customised products in record time and without having to make sacrifices to acquire those products (Kotha 1995).

Prior research suggests that product customisation has a number of different conceptual constructs. For instance, Bardacki and Whitelock (2003) suggest that variety in a product line will make it more likely that each consumer finds the exact option they desire, boosting market share and profitability. In a study of Canadian companies conducting business in Japan, Ryans (1988) found that products that were modified to meet the needs of the Japanese consumer had significantly higher market share than the products that were not. Kahn's idea is central to the argument of product customisation strategy. The more choice an export organisation offers (profitably) to international consumers, the more likely it is to succeed in export markets in the long term. The purpose of this chapter is to gain an understanding of how managerial decision makers make the product customisation decision for export food and beverage products exported to China.

## Nutritional and diet issues

The sweeping economic reforms in China over the past 35 years have resulted in increased disposable incomes and changes to the traditional diet among Chinese people. This has also resulted in changes to nutritional consumption (Popkin 1998; Zimmerman 2011; Zhai et al. 2009). At the same time the status of diet program and nutrition among the city and non-urban communities in China has undergone important enhancement, and the prevalence of malnutrition and nourishment inadequacies has been continuously decreasing (Zhai et al. 2004). Whilst the prevalence of malnutrition and under nutrition has decreased in China, the rate of obesity among the adult population has increased (Wang et al. 2006). The increase in obesity and related chronic diseases is partly attributed to a change in lifestyle among the Chinese population (Monda et al. 2008; Popkin and Du 2003). It is also attributed to a change in diet.

The typical Chinese diet consists of vegetables and cereals, with few animal fats. By world standards this diet is considered healthy when adequate levels of intake are consumed (Zhai et al. 2009). However, with rapid urbanisation and increased hours spent working and therefore less time to cook, the Chinese economic miracle has led to the urban population eating more meals away from the home. This has resulted in an increase in the amount of animal products among the wealthier, urban Chinese consumers (Popkin 2003).

## Reasons for the changing dietary intake and food nutrition

A significant outcome of China's rapid economic development is urbanisation. With that urbanisation comes a transformation in the way packaged food and beverages are distributed. Food distribution, in any nation, is a key component of the overall food system. In China, there has been an enormous penetration of super – and mega-market companies that dominate food distribution in large urban population centres. These large food distribution outlets also have large convenience store chains. The fresh market (wet or open public market) is disappearing as the major source of food throughout the developing world is being replaced by large regional and local supermarkets, which are usually part of multinational chains (e.g. Carrefour or Walmart). Increasingly, hypermarkets (that is, megastores) are the major force driving changes in food expenditures in any country or region Popkin, et al. 2012). The emergence of supermarket retailing in China was supported by a government initiative in 1992 to deregulate the retailing industry by encouraging foreign branded retailers to enter the market (Goldman 2000).

Furthermore, urbanization, with the consequent entry of women in the workforce has increased the opportunity cost of women's time and their incentive to seek shopping convenience and processed foods to save cooking time (Reardon et al. 2003). The traditional food retails have become outdated in their mode of operation (Lo et al. 2001).

Coupled with an increase in supermarket dominance of food and beverage retailing in China, is the fact that Chinese consumers not only have higher disposable incomes, but they are spending more of their income on food (Lo et al. 2001). This has made it attractive for foreign branded food and beverage manufacturers to target China as an export market. Furthermore, given the increasing preference among Chinese urban consumers (in particular) to frequent supermarkets for their food purchases, it is no surprise that there is an imbalance in their nutrition and dietary intake, since supermarket retailers typically market packaged food products that contain, amongst other things, saturated fats, sugar, and food additives.

## What can packaged food and beverage exporters do about it?

In light of the changing dietary habits and nutritional intake among the (mainly) urban Chinese population, what role can packaged food and beverage exporters play in addressing these issues? One could argue that the growing obesity problem in China is not solely related to food intake. This suggests that food manufacturers may have a minimal role to play. Indeed, food and beverage exporters may target several nations for their product, so why focus on any one nation and why China?

Additionally, packaged food manufacturers could strongly argue that they are merely satisfying Chinese consumer needs when they provide products that have limited nutritional value, if that is what the market demands. Thus, they may rightly claim they are simply adhering to the marketing concept. This explanation, whilst valid and logical from one perspective, fails to adhere to the basic tenets of social responsibility. Therefore, when designing their food and beverage products and determining the product's content for the China market, food exporters have a moral responsibility to customise their entire marketing mix, and in particular their product strategy to provide more nutritional content. There are several ways in which food exporters may achieve this. First, traditionally, marketing has been shown to increase the availability of product brands in consumers' minds, to increase preferences for those brands, to increase consumption of those brands, and to increase consumption even of dissimilar foods. The time has come to link consumption with nutrition, not only in the exporters' marketing communication strategies, but in the product content itself. Doing so, helps educate consumers on better eating and links the brand with healthy food consumption. Given the rising cases of obesity related chronic diseases in China, such branding practice may pave the way for competitive advantage for the food exporter.

Second, food exporters can brand their products as a healthy alternative to competing brands by focusing on food consumption as a lifestyle choice not a hunger satisfying vehicle. Doing so reduces the incidence of eating snack foods as a reason for not cooking at home or having to 'eat on the run.' Such practice makes food innovation at the forefront of any new product development strategy for the packaged food exporter. It is also a means by which the manufacturer can segment the market with their offering and differentiate themselves from their competition in the mind of the consumer.

Third, scholars have argued that people over-consume products such as fatty foods, sugary beverages, and salty snacks because they are more palatable than other foods (Drewnoswki 1997; Drewnowski and Specter 2004; Kessler 2010). Food nutrition promotional campaigns, especially at point of sale, that link such products with chronic diseases by demonstrating the necessity of nutrients for a healthy lifestyle are a necessity for packaged food manufacturers. Demonstrating the amount of nutrients a person needs as part of their daily intake and demonstrating how a given branded packaged food item provides that level of nutrition (that is, a customised product) is central to the manufacturers' product development strategy.

Finally, extant research reveals that as advertising for a given packaged food product increases, so does consumption of that product (Brester and Schroeder 1995; Chang and Green 1989; Ward and Dixon 1989). Marketers have two responsibilities in this regard. First, to manufacture nutritionally sound packaged food for Chinese consumers. Second, to communicate the nutritional aspects of the food product in their marketing communications. One way to achieve this is to ensure that healthy aspects of the food product, such as nutrients, are clearly identified on the product's packaging.

**Food packaging and labeling issues**

Nutrition information on food labels is regarded as a major means for encouraging consumers to make healthier choices when shopping for food (Cheftel 2005; Grunert et al. 2010). The substantial number of nutrient and health claims appearing on packaged food labels highlights the importance of understanding how consumers use health claims, in conjunction with nutrition information, to form product evaluations (Kozup et al. 2003). Packaged food and beverage manufacturers have a substantial role to play in how consumers evaluate food products, since packaging is a highly customisable aspect of any product. This strategic approach should not be the sole responsibility of the food manufacturer. A coordinated customisation approach throughout the entire food chain is required (Hawkes 2008).

The sale of food products in China (as they are elsewhere in the world) are governed by regulations. Whilst other countries have been quick to embrace the World Health Organisation's Global Strategy on Diet, Physical Activity and Health as a means by which to reduce diet related diseases, China has been slower to embrace this initiative. Further, despite attempts by governments to ensure that packaged food and beverage manufacturers include nutritional information on their goods' labels, the amount of academic research into consumers' use of labels for nutritional information is still relatively scarce (Drichoutis et al. 2006). This raises an important question: what factors influence consumers' label usage as sources of nutritional information? Answering this question enables packaged food manufacturers to better tailor (customise) their labels to ensure not only the correct amount nutritional information appears on the product's labelling (which in China, is mandated by law), but also that any supporting marketing communications campaign aimed at explaining the nutritional value of a food or beverage product is appropriately directed to the right consumer(s).

In trying to understand the use of product labelling as a source of informed nutritional value of a packaged food product, Wang et al. (1995) found that household size is an important determinant. Wang et al. (1995) posit that larger households are more likely to use labels than smaller households. Further, Wang et al. (1995) and Nayga et al. (1998) suggest that the educational level of the primary buyer of packaged foods for household consumption is an important determinant of label use. The more educated the buyer, the more likely they are to refer to the label's nutrition information. Mueller (1991) suggest that the more health conscious a consumer is, the more likely they are to obtain their food nutrition information for a product's label. A study by Navder (1993) found that nutrition labels are the most used source of nutrition information. She suggests that food labels should be more informative to consumers. The nutrition information provided on the label may be the only source of information available to the consumer at the point of purchase, so it is important that they are able to understand and use this information to guide their food selection (Cowburn and Stockley 2005). Apart from the legal obligation of including nutritional information on labels, how else can packaged food exporters targeting China customise their packaging and labelling to provide additional information?

One suggested product customisation strategy for connecting consumers with the nutritional information on a product's labelling, is to simplify the language used on the labels. Consumers are unlikely to make nutritional choices, if labelling is contains nutritional information that is difficult to understand. Too often, health science and food technology jargon whilst trying to inform the consumers has the effect of diluting the health message. Further, the amount of information on a package is often constrained by the package size.

Understanding the nutrition information found on a product's label suggests that consumers recognise and understand nutrient terms and that they understand the relationships between different nutrients and the role of each nutrient in the body and in terms of healthy eating (Cowburn and Stockley 2005). This is not always the case. Yet, packaged food manufacturers seldom link the nutrients in a product to a balanced diet and healthy eating. Further, extant research reveals that nutritional knowledge may not adequately predict dietary behaviour, because consumers with dietary knowledge do not necessarily change their behaviour (Bernues et al. 2003; Drichoutis et al. 2005; Sapp 1991; Shepherd and Towler 1992). Sometime it's a case of consumers not understanding the information they read (Capps, 1992). What's the point of customising the product's packaging to explain the nutritional value of a packaged food product, if consumers routinely ignore the contents of the labeling, or don't understand what they are reading? Indeed, adjunct questions include: Do Chinese consumers really want nutritional information? Having acquired the nutritional information, how likely are these consumers to use it (Nayga et al. 1998)? Regardless of the answers to these questions, packaged food manufactures have a moral, ethical, and usually a legal obligation to customise their product packaging in a manner that provides not only the requisite amount of nutritional information, but also the way the nutritional ingredients are link to diet and healthy living.

## Country of origin and food product customisation: The China view

The relaxation of trade policies, specifically the reduction of import tariffs under the influence of globalisation, has provided consumers with more foreign product choices than ever before. Chinese consumers are subject to this increased choice. Consequently, their attitudes towards products originating from foreign countries are of interest to international business and consumer behaviour researchers (Wang and Chen 2004).

Liberalisation of world markets has driven many organisations to internationalize their marketing activities to survive and grow. Success internationally clearly depends on the acceptability of products by consumers in different countries (Kaynak et al. 2000). Products may be linked to a country by virtue of its location, weather, and natural resources or because of traditional manufacturing expertise (Usunier and Cestre 2007). In addition, products may be linked to countries because the particular country is known for its product innovation and development. Within a China context, extant research reveal that Chinese consumers weigh a product's country of origin heavily, but perceive a product made outside of China as a strong positive stimulus or attribute to consider while making selection and purchasing decisions (McDonald 1995).

## The importance of country of origin research

Country of origin is one of the oldest and most common research topics in international business. Extant research reveals that a products country of origin can serve as a signal of product quality (Li and Dwyer 1994). Further, country of origin can positively affect a product's perceived value and customers' purchase intention (Knight and Calantone, 2000). Country of origin perceptions can encompass an entire country's manufactured products. Not surprisingly then, many marketing practitioners will argue that country of origin stereotyping plays a vital part in their marketing strategies (Colyer 2005). However, as Balestrini and Gamble (2006) report, for certain products consumers may be less inclined to use country of origin information, whilst Hugstad and Durr (1986) found that sensitivity to country of origin varies by product category but is highest for durable goods. From a food and beverage product perspective, the perception of a product's origin and the presentation of origin information in a retail environment can have a great influence on sales (Chaney 2002). It can influence both the nature of its international marketing strategy and the way in which consumer purchasing decisions are made (Balestrini and Gamble 2006). A product's geographic origin not only is a cognitive cue for judgments about product quality, but also has affective (emotional) and normative (relating to personal and social norms) connotations (Verlegh and van Ittersum, 2001). However, consumers cannot easily observe many food characteristics such as origin, means of production, or taste (Ehmke et al. 2008). This poses a great challenge for packaged food exporters when customising their product. How do they customise their product in a manner that makes it easier for international consumers to discern and infer, for example, quality?

In trying to understand the scope of country of origin effects on an exporter targeting China with their packaged food and beverage products, it is important to note that country of origin effects are iterative, that is they can have both positive and negative effects. For instance, country of origin effects among Chinese consumers may be positive for one product category, whilst negative for another. Where do the imported packaged food and beverage product categories fit into this paradigm? Perhaps a starting put is to consider the parameters of the country of origin affects. As Knight et al. (2007) suggest, country image can act as only one of several extrinsic cues that buyers use to perceive quality of products or services. Thus, in the minds of consumers, country of origin affects work alongside other extrinsic cues (e.g. price). To explain this, Monroe (2003: 160) offers: "generally, buyers are likely to use cues that are high in predictive value and high in confidence value to assess quality".

Contrary to customer durables, foodstuffs are in common bought with low participation on the part of the customer. Impulse buying or unexpected buying performs an important part in customer behaviour (Beatty and Ferrell 1998), probably accounting for more than 50 per cent of the shopping products bought (Phillips and Bradshaw 1993). Research has shown that "the first flavour is almost always with the eye", indicating that visible hints, such as product packaging and colour, significantly impact a consumer's preliminary approval of a packaged food product (Imran 1999). However, "food is both content and icon, content and aesthetic" (Marshall 1995: 3), so many factors other than overall look and flavour come into play. Cardello 1996: 232) suggests "the hedonic sizing natural in meals can be found at the centre of meals acceptance". Many of the impacts of meals choice are mediated by personal values and behaviour, such as aspects that figure out self-identity, for example, identity with sustainable consumerism (Shepherd and Raats 1996). Clearly, then culture plays an important role in consumers' decision making regarding food products. As such, an understanding of Chinese consumers' personal values and their effect on purchasing foreign branded food products is an integral part of a packaged food manufacturer's new product development for China.

Chinese consumers not having access to foreign branded products until 1978 may explain why Chinese consumers have a strong preference for foreign brands (Sin et al. 2000). This view is supported by the rapid influx of foreign products and brands entering the Chinese market (Bates 1998). Foreign brands are those originating from Western economies, although large amounts also originate from Asian nations, predominantly from Japan. The consumption of foreign brands is especially high for Chinese consumers living in the major cities and who are relatively affluent, young, and educated (Dickson et al. 2004). This has been explained by the preference of Chinese consumers for the symbolic benefits associated with foreign brands (Zhou and Hui 2003). Chinese consumers have traditionally associated foreign brands with concepts of sophistication, prestige, modernity, and novelty. Furthermore, foreign brands are traditionally perceived in China as having higher quality (Li et al. 1997).

## Country of origin and food labelling

Consumers cannot easily observe the national origin of food on a retail shelf. This suggests that a food product's national origin is an unobservable credence attribute that creates an asymmetric information problem that can lead to product failure (Akerlof 1970). A solution to this problem is created when packaged food manufacturers provide consumers with complete symmetric information by means of product labelling. This labelling can be customised for a country by country basis and if needed, on a product by product basis.

Consumers' taste evaluations are influenced by cultural symbols ascribed, consciously or unconsciously, to a food or beverage often depicted in a product's labeling. Kotler (1997) provides packaged food exporters with a practical guide to the aims of labeling. He states that food product labeling has four functions: To identify, grade, describe and promote the product. These functions enhance the ability to differentiate products, enlarge product attractiveness and assure the customer of a certain level of product quality (Northen 2000). Each of these elements is highly customisable during the design stage of the new product development process. Given that labels carry useful nutritional, dietary, and product usage information, customising packaged food product labels to reflect language differences between the export product's country of origin and China is a mandatory product customisation strategy. This matter is complicated by the linguistic diversity within China.

## Country of origin and branding

An alternative way to look at country of origin and its effect on the packaged food product customisation decision is to consider the notion of country of *association* (Li et al. 2000). In other words, consumers will have an image of Lamborghini as an Italian car (even though it is not owned by an Italian company) and Nike products are seen as American (even when they are produced in China) (Josiassen and Harzing 2008). As such, country of origin is increasingly considered as that country which consumers typically associate with a brand, "irrespective of where it is actually manufactured" (Usunier, 2006: 62). Clearly then, as Josiassen and Harzing (2008) assert, if the country of *association* is the relevant country of origin that is considered by consumers and managed by companies, then it is less relevant whether consumers are (made) aware of the manufacturing origin of the product. How do packaged food exporters factor this into their branding strategy for China? One approach is to consider the careful selection of brand names. Ahmed, d'Astous and Zoutien (1993) found that the brand name explained the largest proportion of variance in product quality rating among consumers. Thus brand names provide product developers an opportunity to differentiate themselves through brand names (Michell, King and Reast 2001), as they may carry positive associations that affect how consumers perceive and evaluate the foreign branded products Leclerc et al. 1994). Consider for example, Haagen Dazs ice cream. It's a United States owned brand with a distinctive Scandinavian sounding brand name. The aim of product origin in new product development management is *not* to ensure that consumers have objectively accurate knowledge of the actual origin of a product; it is to manage the stereotypical images of product origins that consumers form (Josiassen and Harzing, 2008). This view is supported by Supanvanij and Amine (2000) who posit that brand name products with an unfavorable country of origin image do not lose its advantage compared to the brand name products with a favorable country of origin image. The no-name product with a favorable country-of-origin image can offset the disadvantage of not being the brand name product. Management of these brand-country images occurs through the customisation of the brand for specific international markets.

Both country of origin and brand name of a product are extrinsic product cues that are distinct from a physical product characteristic or intrinsic attribute. Although, neither brand name nor country of origin has a direct bearing on product performance, combined they can affect the consumer's perception of the product's quality, style, and expected price (Supanvanij and Amine, 2000). Is branding really that important to Chinese consumers? Yang (1989) found that

Chinese consumers are in a low involvement purchase situation when products are used for private consumption and typically consumed at home. They are likely to adopt a rather simple cognitive stance, favoring the physical functions of the product and being mostly concerned with price and quality. In contrast, there is a high level of product involvement among the Chinese consumers buy products for their social symbolic value. It was asserted that when purchasing for home consumption, Chinese consumers tend to focus their purchasing decisions on the price of a product and buy whatever is the least expensive. Conversely, China's history may tell a different consumption story. China evolved from a feudal society where a person's status in the hierarchy is demonstrated through the concept of 'face'. Thus, if a person can afford an expensive imported (i.e. foreign branded) product, this shows others that the person has succeeded economically (Anderson and He, 1998). This may explain why expensive bottles of imported red wine have become the latest "trophy drink" of the newly rich Chinese who like to drink such wines when eating out, in order to show they are successful and have both the money and good taste to be wine drinkers (Hu et al. 2008). Given these contradictory finding, the export food product customisation imperative takes on an even greater significance during the new product development stage.

## Conclusion

Consumers select products they believe best satisfy their needs. Research has shown that the decisive factor in consumers' food and beverage product choice is taste. In turn, marketers, through their new product development process attempt to develop offers that best match their consumers' taste requirements. The development of such offers is impacted by cultural differences in consumer needs, tastes, and demands. To that end, new product development across international borders becomes a more complex proposition for international marketing organisations.

One of the key managerial decisions facing organisations engaging in new product development is knowing how much to customise a product sold in their domestic market, for one or more export markets. This managerial decision has both product and brand performance implications. Many factors will impact such a managerial decision.

Product customisation has become an important strategic choice for packaged food exporters. An organisation's agility and quick responsiveness to changes in world markets, especially China with her rapidly developing economy, have become mandatory in view of current levels of market globalization, rapid technological innovations, and intense competition. Packaged food product customisation broadly encompasses the ability to provide individually-designed products to meet the market needs, encompassing the diverse consumer tastes, desire to purchase foreign made or branded products, and overall attitude towards nutrition.

To succeed in exporting packaged foods to China, manufacturers, as part of their new product development processes must investigate how export market characteristics such as local government regulation, infrastructure differences, cultural differences, end□ user differences in tastes and preferences, and competitive intensity affect ideal product adaptation.

## References

Ahmed, S. A., D' Astous, A., and Zoutien, S. (1993). Personality Variables and the "Made In" Concept. In Papadopoulos, N. and L. Heslop (Ed.), *Product-Country Images, Impact and Role in International Marketing*. Binghampton: The Hawthorne Press, Inc.

Akerlof, G. A. (1970). The Market for 'Lemons': Quality Uncertainty and the Market Mechanism. *Quarterly Journal of Economics, 84* (3), 488-500.

Anderson, P.M. and He, X. (1998). Price influence and age segments of Beijing consumers. *Journal of Consumer Marketing, 15* (2), 152-69.

Bai, J., Wahl, T. I., Lohmar, B. T., and Huang, J. (2010). Food away from home in Beijing: Effects of wealth, time and "free" meals. *China Economic Review, 21* (3), 432-441.

Balestrini, P., and Gamble, P. (2006). Country-of-origin effects on Chinese wine consumers. *British Food Journal, 108* (5), 396-412.

Bates, C. (1998). The many China markets. *The China Business Review*, September-October, 26-32.

Bardacki, A., and Whitelock, J. (2003). Mass customisation in marketing: The consumer perspective. *Journal of Consumer Marketing, 20* (5), 463-479.

Beatty, S. and Ferrell, S. (1998). Impulse buying: modelling its precursors. *Journal of Retailing 74* (2), 169–192.

Bernués, A., Olaizola, A., and Corcoran, K. (2003). Labelling information demanded by European consumers and relationships with purchasing motives, quality and safety of meat. *Meat Science, 65* (3), 1095-1106.

Buatsi, S. N. (1986). Organisational Adaptation in International Marketing. *International Marketing Review*, 3 (Winter), 17-26.

Boddewyn, J.J., Soehl, R, and Piccard, J. (1986). Standardization in international marketing: is Theodore Levitt in fact right? *Business Horizons* (November-December), 69-75.

Brester, G. W., and Schroeder, T. C. (1995). The impacts of brand and generic advertising on meat demand. *American Journal of Agricultural Economics,77* (4), 969-979.

Calantone, R. J., and Knight, G. (2000). The critical role of product quality in the international performance of industrial firms. *Industrial Marketing Management, 29* (493-506).

Capps, O. (1992). Consumer response to changes in food labeling: discussion. American *Journal of Agricultural Economics, 74* (5), 1215–1216.

Cardello, A.V. (1996). The Role of the Human Senses in Food Acceptance, in H.L. Meiselman and H.J.H. MacFie (eds.), *Food Choice, Acceptance and Consumption*, Blackie Academic: London, pp. 51–52.

Cavusgil, T. S., Zou, S. and Naidu, GM. (1993). Product and promotion adaptation in export ventures: An empirical investigation. *Journal of International Business Studies, 24* (3), 479-501.

Chadee, D. D., Qiu, F., and Rose, E. (2003). FDI Location at the Sub-National Level: A Study of EJVs in China. *Journal of Business Research*, 56 (10), 835-845.

Chamon, M., and De Carvalho Filho, I. (2014). Consumption based estimates of urban Chinese growth. *China Economic Review, 29* (June), 126-137.

Chaney, I.M. (2002). Promoting wine by country. *International Journal of Wine Marketing, 14* (1). 34-40.

Chang, H. S., and Green, R. (1989). The effects of advertising on food demand elasticities. *Canadian Journal of Agricultural Economics, 37* (3), 481-494.

Cheftel, J. C. (2005). Food and nutrition labelling in the European Union. *Food Chemistry, 93,* 531–550.

Colyer, Edwin. (2005). Beer brands and homelands. Accessed 2014 (12th July ).

Cowburn, G.,and Stockley, L. (2005). Consumer understanding and use of nutrition labelling: a systematic review. Public Health Nutrition, 8 (1), 21-28.

Datt, G. (1999). Has poverty declined since economic reforms? Statistical data analysis. Economic and Political Weekly, 59 (12), 3516-3518.

Davis, D. S. (2000). China's consumer revolution. Current History, 99 (638), 248-254.

Denton, L. T. and X. Kaixuan (1995). Food Selection and Consumption in Chinese Markets: An Overview. Journal of International Food and Agribusiness Marketing, 7 (1), 55-77.

Dickson, M., Lennon, S., Montalto, C., Shen, D. and Zhang, L. (2004). Chinese consumer market segments for foreign apparel products. Journal of Consumer Marketing, 21 (5), 301-17.

Drewnowski A. (1997). Taste preferences and food intake. Annual Review Nutrition. 17, 237–53

Drewnowski A,. and Specter S.E. (2004). Poverty and obesity: the role of energy density and energy costs. American Journal of Clinical Nutrition. 79 (1), 6–16

Drichoutis, A. C., Lazaridis, P., and Nayga, R. M. (2005). Nutrition knowledge and consumer use of nutritional food labels. European Review of Agricultural Economics, 32 (1), 93-118.

Drichoutis, A., Lazaridis, P., and Nayga Jr, R. M. (2006). Consumers' use of nutritional labels: a review of research studies and issues. Academy of Marketing Science Review, 10 (9).

Ehmke, M. D., Lusk, J. L., and Tyner, W. (2008). Measuring the relative importance of preferences for country of origin in China, France, Niger, and the United States. Agricultural Economics, 38 (3), 277-285.

Escalas, J. E., and Bettman, J. R. (2003). You Are What They Eat: The Influence of Reference Groups on Consumers' Connections to Brands. Journal of Consumer Psychology, 13 (3), 339-348.

Gale, F. and Huang, K. (2007). Demand for Food Quantity Quality in China (No. 32).

Goldman, A. (2000). Supermarkets in China: the case of Shanghai. The International Review of Retail, Distribution and Consumer Research, 10 (1), 1-21.

Grunert, K. G., Wills, J. M., and Fernández-Celemín, L. (2010). Nutrition knowledge, and use and understanding of nutrition information on food labels among consumers in the UK. Appetite, 55 (2), 177-189.

Hawkes, C. (2008). Agro□ food industry growth and obesity in China: What role for regulating food advertising and promotion and nutrition labelling? Obesity Reviews, 9 (S1), 151-161.

Hu, X., Li, L., Xie, C., and Zhou, J. (2008). The effects of country-of-origin on Chinese consumers' wine purchasing behaviour. Journal of Technology Management in China, 3 (3), 292-306.

Hugstad, P., and M. Durr. (1986). A Study of Country of Manufacturer Impact on Consumer Perceptions. In Developments in Marketing Science. Miami: Academy of Marketing Science, 1986.

Huang, J., Li, N., and Rozelle, S. (2003). Trade reform, household effects, and poverty in rural China. American Journal of Agricultural Economics, 85 (5), 1292-1298.

Imran, N. (1999). The role of visual cues in consumer perception and acceptance of a food product. Nutrition and Food Science 99 (5), 224–229.

Josiassen, A., and Harzing, A. W. (2008). Comment: Descending from the ivory tower: reflections on the relevance and future of country□ of□ origin research. European Management Review, 5 (4), 264-270.

Jussaume, R. A. (2001). Factors Associated with Modern Urban Chinese Food

Consumption Patterns. Journal of Contemporary China. 10 (27), 219-232.

Kahn, B. (1998). Dynamic relationships with customers: High-variety strategies.

Journal of the Academy of Marketing Science, 26 (1), 45-53.

Kaynak, E., Kucukemiroglu, O. and Hyder, A.S. (2000). Consumers' country-of-origin (COO) perceptions of imported products in a homogeneous less-developed country, European Journal of Marketing, 34, 9/10, 1221-41.

Kessler D. (2010). The End of Overeating: Taking Control of the Insatiable American Appetite. Emmaus, PA: Rodale

Knight, J. G., Holdsworth, D. K., and Mather, D. W. (2007). Country-of-origin and choice of food imports: an in-depth study of European distribution channel gatekeepers. Journal of International Business Studies, 38 (1), 107-125.

Kogut, B. (1985). Designing Global Strategies: Profiting from Operational Efficiency. Sloan Management Review, 26 (Fall), 27-38.

Kotha, S. (1995). Mass Customization: Implementing The Emerging Paradigm For Competitive Advantage, Strategic Management Journal, 16, 21-42.

Kotler, P. (1986). Global Standardization: Courting Danger. Journal of Consumer Marketing, 3 (Spring), 13–15

Kotler, P. (1997). Marketing Management: Analysis, Planning, Implementation, and Control. Englewood Cliffs: Prentice-Hall International.

Kotler, P., and Keller, K. L. (2012). *Marketing Management* (14 ed.). Upper Saddle River, NJ: Prentice Hall.

Kozup, J. C., Creyer, E. H., and Burton, S. (2003). Making healthful food choices: The influence of health claims and nutrition information on consumers' evaluations of packaged food products and restaurant menu items. *Journal of Marketing*, 67 (2), 19-34.

Landwehr, J. R., Wentzel, D., and Herrmann, A. (2012). The Tipping Point of Design: How Product Design and Brands Interact to Affect Consumers' Preferences. *Psychology and Marketing*, 29 (6), 422-433.

Leclerc, F., Schmitt, B. H., and Dubé, L. (1994). Foreign branding and its effects on product perceptions and attitudes. *Journal of Marketing Research*. 31 (2), 263-270.

Leonidou, L.C. (1996). Product standardization or adaptation: the Japanese approach. Journal of Marketing Practice, 2 (4), 53-71.

Levitt, T. (1983). The globalization of markets. Harvard Business Review, 61 (May-June), 92-102.

Li, Z.G., Murray, L.W., and Scott, D. (2000). Global sourcing, multiple country of origin facets, and consumer reactions. Journal of Business Research, 47 (2): 121-33.

Li, L., Yong, H.-H., Borland, R., Fong, G. T., Thompson, M. E., Jiang, Y., Yang, Y., Sirirassame, B., Hastings, G., and Harris, F. (2009). Reported Awareness of Tobacco Advertising and Promotion in China Compared to Thailand, Australia and the USA. Tobacco Control, 18, 222-227.

Li, W.K., and Dwyer, R.S. Jnr. (1994). The Role of Country of Origin in Product Evaluations: Informational and Standard of Comparison Effects. Journal of Consumer Psychology, 3 (2), 187-212

Li, Z., Fu, S. and Murray, L. (1997). Country and product images: the perceptions of consumers in the People's Republic of China, Journal of International Consumer Marketing, 10 (1/2), 115-39.

Lo, T. W. C., Lau, H. F., & Lin, G. S. (2001). Problems and prospects of supermarket development in China. International Journal of Retail & Distribution Management, 29 (2), 66-76.

Luo, Y. (2007). From Foreign Investors to Strategic Insiders: Shifting Parameters, Prescriptions and Paradigms for MNCs in China. Journal of World Business, 42 (1), 14-34.

Marshall, D.W. (ed.) (1995). Food Choice and the Consumer. Blackie Academic & Professional: London.

McDonald, J. (1995). Chinese prefer to buy from their own. San Francisco Examiner,

Maheswaran, D. (1994). Country-of-origin as a stereotype: effects on consumer expertise and attribute strength on product evaluations. Journal of Consumer Research, 21 (2). 354-65.

Michell, P., King, J., and Reast, J. (2001). Brand values related to industrial products. Industrial marketing management, 30 (5), 415-425.

Monda, K. L., Adair, L. S., Zhai, F., and Popkin, B. M. (2008). Longitudinal relationships between occupational and domestic physical activity patterns and body weight in China. European Journal of Clinical Nutrition, 62 (11), 1318-1325.

Monroe, K.B. (2003) Pricing: Making Profitable Decisions, 3rd edn, McGraw-Hill Irwin: Boston, MA.

Mueller, W. (1991). Who read the label? American Demographics, 13 (January), 36-41.

Navder, K. P. (1995). Food and Nutrition Labeling: Past, Present, and Future. Journal of Home Economics, 85 (Summer), 43-50.

Nayga, R. M., Lipinski, D., and Savur, N. (1998). Consumers' use of nutritional labels while food shopping and at home. Journal of Consumer Affairs, 32 (1), 106-120.

Northen, J. R. (2000). Quality attributes and quality cues Effective communication in the UK meat supply chain. British Food Journal. 102 (3), 230-245.

Ohmae, K. (1985). Triad Power: The Coming Shape of Global Competition, The Free Press, New York, NY.

Phillips, H. and Bradshaw, R. (1993). How customers actually shop: customer interaction with the point of sale. Journal of the Market Research Society, 35 (1): 51–62.

Popkin, B. M. (1998). The nutrition transition and its health implications in lower-income countries. Public Health Nutrition, 1 (1), 5-21.

Popkin, B. M. (2003). The nutrition transition in the developing world. Development Policy Review, 21 (5□ 6), 581-597.

Popkin, B. M., Adair, L. S., and Ng, S. W. (2012). Global nutrition transition and the pandemic of obesity in developing countries. Nutrition Reviews, 70 (1), 3-21.

Reardon, T., Timmer, C. P., Barrett, C. B., and Berdegué, J. (2003). The rise of supermarkets in Africa, Asia, and Latin America. American journal of agricultural economics, 85 (5), 1140-1146.

Regmi, A. and Gehlhar, M. (2005). New Directions in Global Food Markets, USDA.

Roth, A. V., Tsay, A.A., Pullman, M. E., and Gray, J. V. (2008). Unravelling the Food Supply Chain. Strategic Insights from China. Journal of Supply Chain Management. 44 (1), 22-39.

Sapp, S. G. (1991). Impact of nutritional knowledge within an expanded rational expectations model of beef consumption. Journal of Nutrition Education, 23 (5), 214-222.

Schuh, A. (2000). Global standardization as a success formula for marketing in Central Eastern Europe. Journal of World Business, 35 (2), 133-148.

Shepherd, R. and Raats, M.M. (1996). Attitudes and Beliefs in Food Habits, in H.L. Meiselman and H.J.H. MacFie (eds.), Food Choice Acceptance and Consumption, Blackie Academic: London, pp: 346–364.

Shepherd, R., and Towler, G. (1992). Nutrition knowledge, attitudes and fat intake: application of the theory of reasoned action. Journal of Human Nutrition and Dietetics, 5 (6), 387-397.

Sin, L., Ho, S.C. and So, S. (2000). Research on advertising in Mainland China: a review and assessment. Asia Pacific Journal of Marketing and Logistics, 12 (1), 37-65.

Siraliova, J., and Angelis, J. J. (2006). Marketing Strategy in the Baltics: Standardise or Adapt? Baltic Journal of Management, 1 (2), 169-187.

Sridhar, K. S., and Wan, G. (2010). Firm location choice in cities: Evidence from China, India, and Brazil. China Economic Review, 21(1), 113-122.

Summers, L. (2007). The Rise of Asia and the Global Economy. Research Monitor (the bi-annual newsletter of the Global Development Network), Special Issue: 4–5.

Usunier, Jean-Claude. (2006). Relevance in business research: the case of country-of-origin research in marketing. European Management Review, 3 (1): 60-73.

Usunier, J. C., and Cestre, G. (2007). Product Ethnicity: Revisiting the Match Between Products and Countries. Journal of International Marketing, 15 (3), 32-72.

Valenzuela, A., and Dhar, R. (2004). Effects of preference elicitation task on consumer reactions to product customization. Advances in Consumer Research, 31, 685-688.

Veeck, A. and Burns, A. C. (2005) Changing Tastes: The Adoption of New Food Choices in Post-Reform China. Journal of Business Research, 5 (4), 644-652.

Verlegh, P.W.J. and van Ittersum, K. (2001). The Origin of the Spices: The Impact of Geographic Product Origin on Consumer Decision Making. In L. Frewer, E. Risvik and H. Schifferstein (eds.), Food, People and Society, Springer: Berlin, pp: 267–279.

Wang, G., Fletcher, S. M., and Carley, D. H. (1995). Consumer utilization of food labeling as a source of nutrition information. Journal of Consumer Affairs, 29 (2), 368-380.

Wang, C. L., and Chen, Z. X. (2004). Consumer ethnocentrism and willingness to buy domestic products in a developing country setting: testing moderating effects. Journal of Consumer Marketing, 21 (6), 391-400.

Wang, Y., Mi, J., Shan, X. Y., Wang, Q. J., and Ge, K. Y. (2006). Is China facing an obesity epidemic and the consequences? The trends in obesity and chronic disease in China. International Journal of Obesity, 31 (1), 177-188.

Ward, R. W., and Dixon, B. L. (1989). Effectiveness of fluid milk advertising since the Dairy and Tobacco Adjustment Act of 1983. American Journal of Agricultural Economics, 71 (3), 730-740.

Wei, Y. D., and Leung, C. K. (2005). Development Zones, Foreign Investment, and Global City Formation in Shanghai. Growth and Change, 36 (1), 16-40.

World Bank (2011). World Development Indicators 2011. Washington, DC: World Bank.

Yang, M.C. (1989). Feminism and Chinese national character, in Lee, Y.Y. and Yang, K.S. (Eds), Symposium on the Character of the Chinese, Institute of Ethnology, Academia Sinica.

Yip, G. S. (2003). Total Global Strategy, Prentice Hall, Englewood Cliffs, NJ.

Zhai, F. Y., Wang, H. J., Chang, S. Y., Fu, D., Ge, K., and Popkin, B. M. (2004). The current status, trend, and influencing factors to malnutrition of infants and children in China. Journal of Community Nutrition, 6 (2), 78-85.

Zhai, F., Wang, H., Du, S., He, Y., Wang, Z., Ge, K., and Popkin, B. M. (2009). Prospective study on nutrition transition in China. Nutrition Reviews, 67 (S1), S56-S61.

Zhou, J. X., Arnold, M. J., Pereira, A., and Yu, J. (2010). Chinese Consumer Decision-Making Styles: A Comparison Between the Coastal and Inland Regions. Journal of Business Research, 63 (1), 45-51.

Zhou, L. and Hui, M. (2003). Symbolic value of foreign products in the People's Republic of China. Journal of International Marketing, 11 (2), 36-58.

Zimmerman, F. J. (2011). Using Marketing Muscle to Sell Fat: The Rise of Obesity in the Modern Economy. Annual Review of Public Health, 32, 285–306.

# 6

# Food: A non-traditional challenge to security

**Rita Parker**

## Introduction

Food security is a complex notion which is dependent on an equally complex set of variables and actors that can influence the production, quality, availability, supply chain, affordability and use of food for each nationstate and its civil society. Demand for resources of all kinds is likely to increase into the future as the world's population rises to around ten billion around 2045. While the demand for food is expected to grow, some countries are likely to experience significant declines in agricultural productivity. This will increase pressure on the ability of nation states to meet the needs of their population groups.

Most academic literature and policy focus relies on the 1996 World Food Summit (WFS) definition of food security as existing when 'all people at all times have access to sufficient, safe, nutritious food to maintain a healthy and active life'. This definition is based on the notion of food and its security from a particular perspective which the World Health Organization (WHO) describes as being founded on three pillars namely, food availability, food access, and food use. These three pillars are associated with whether there is sufficient food available on a consistent basis; if there are sufficient resources to obtain appropriate foods for a nutritious diet; and if there is adequate knowledge of basic nutrition and care, as well as adequate water and sanitation associated with food use.

This comprehensive definition is relevant and important within its prescribed context. However, this chapter suggests that the notion of food security when looked at from a complex systems perspective could be reframed to be more inclusive of other issues associated with food and its security, particularly as these other factors and actors have wider implications for a nationstate's overall security as well as the well-being of its civil society.

This chapter examines the notion of food as a nontraditional challenge to security, particularly to human security as well as to that of individual nationstates. It does this by considering the World Food Summit definition of food security against a range of other factors such as threats by nonstate actors and risks from non-human sources. This chapter seeks to explore some of these issues in a more holistic way from an international relations perspective beyond the WHO parameters using complex adaptive systems theory as the analytical framework for this chapter. From a systems perspective, a complex adaptive system is one where we allow for multidimensionality; emergent properties and learning. By adopting a broader perspective it is possible to address those issues which could lead to food *in*security as well as security.

The WHO definition provides a basis to examine some of the broader issues which impact food and its security. For example, availability and access to food are affected by population growth, demographic trends, economic development, government policies, income levels, health, nutrition, gender, environmental degradation, natural disasters, refugees, migration, disease, concentrated resource ownership and conflict. These are transnational issues that are generally blind to sovereign borders as they spread starvation, environmental degradation, and instability across the globe.

## Framing concepts

The way in which policy issues are framed is a key determinant of the responsiveness of the political system. Framing in this sense is a simple analytical idea, denoting what is considered to be important (within the frame) and what is considered to be unimportant (outside the frame). Each frame suggests a different causal pathway and proposes different actors as valid policy participants.

As noted above, the Food and Agriculture Organization (FAO) definition of food security in 1996 is framed around its availability, access, use and stability. For a long time, food security policies were in the domain of agencies dedicated to agricultural use and management. However, the topic of food and its security has been reframed over time and responsibility for it has expanded from being addressed only in specialised fora such as international food and food production organisations. Food security is now being included in the broader spectrum of governance policies and mechanisms such as the G20 forum.

As a result of the global food price crisis in 2008, individual nationstates recognised the threat to international markets and political stability, consequently, in 2010 the G20 leaders agreed to include food security as part of its agenda. The FAO has continued to encourage the G20 to keep the issue of food security on its agenda. The 2011 G20 Summit led to steps to reduce price volatility including the creation of the Excessive Food Price Variability Early Warning System. Its purpose is to alert policymakers when world markets are experiencing a period of excessive food price volatility. This information can then be used to determine appropriate country-level food security responses, such as the release of physical food stocks. The 2011 G20 also established the Agricultural Market Information System (AMIS), to enhance food market transparency and encourage coordination of policy action in response to market uncertainty. The initial focus of AMIS is on four crops that are particularly important in international food markets, namely wheat, maize, rice and soybeans. According to the AMIS, G20 countries produce 80 per cent of the world's rice and China is the world's biggest rice producer and consumer.

The food crisis in the Horn of Africa highlighted the extent of food insecurity and, as a result, the 2011 G20 meetings paid particular attention to the issues of high food prices, food price volatility, and food insecurity. The 2014 G20 in Australia has included the issue of food security as part of its agenda. The elevation of food security issues to the G20 forum underscores the importance individual nationstates place on food and recognises that it is directly linked to issues associated with political and sovereign stability as well as the well-being of individuals.

## Reframing food policies

Linking the concept of food to security reflects that these separate terms have changed and have been reframed over time and, as a result, have become more complex. The concept of food security has evolved over several decades. For example, in the 1970s food policy emphasised an economics approach with its focus on increased production to achieve reliable food supplies particularly for deficit states. As noted by Stringer, most studies during this period tended to define food as cereals, and consequently record low levels of cereal stocks and corresponding high prices raised concerns about the global food system. During this period, the debate focused primarily on the ability of nationstates to produce sufficient food to feed an increasing global population. The limits of growth debate and environmental limitations were an important theme in the early 1970s following the first Earth Day. The 1974 World Food Summit (WFS) conference sought to address the growing perception of increasing food shortage and set out to develop mechanisms to protect food supplies from major crop failures. The WFS at that time defined food security as "the availability at all times of adequate world supplies of basic foodstuffs to sustain a steady expansion of food consumption and to offset fluctuations in production and prices".

In the 1980s the focus of food policies shifted. The debate also began to move away from a focus on global and national food supplies, to a broader frame which included access by individuals who depended on access to resources, technology, markets, social networks and food transfer programs. Consideration was also given to issues associated with vulnerability and entitlement at a household and individual level where access did not depend just on food supply, but related to equitable access to land and income opportunities.

Following the African famines of the 1980s, food was reframed in 'humanitarian' terms. At the time, a series of droughts wiped out harvests followed by a lack of rain and disease which further destroyed crops. By March 1984, the Ethiopian Government warned that five million people were at risk from starvation because the country could produce only 6.2 million tonnes of grain a year, one million less than needed. The situation was complicated by Ethiopia's 20-year civil war in the northern provinces of Eritrea and Tigre. This affected the delivery of aid supplies across the country and there were reports that EEC food was being diverted from civilian famine victims to feed troops. By December that year, international aid had begun to flow, but the Ethiopian government was expanding its internal war and continued to divert aid supplies to its troops. The situation was further exacerbated by heavy storms which flattened the few crops that had been planted. Thousands of refugees were fleeing war and famine and heading into neighbouring Sudan; an estimated 2,000 people a day by December 1984. Throughout 1985, international aid was flown into Ethiopia and the situation began to ease although drought and famine are recurrent problems in that Region. The African famines demonstrate the link between the availability of food and the security of a nationstate and it directly affects the human security of individuals.

Between 1990 and 2000, global food supply was relatively stable. However, the 2008 food riots in 48 nationstates following severe commodity price increases highlighted that policy decisions by individual nationstates were not sufficient to prevent major imbalances between nationstates and among vulnerable population groups. The riots also reaffirmed the links between food security, development and broader security. They further underscored that uncoordinated short-term national policies could result in destabilising global impacts on prices and access to food in other nationstates. Here we see the way food, its production, and availability, becomes increasingly related to national and global security concerns.

It was not until 1996 that the definition of food security, noted at the beginning of this Chapter, began to reflect a more holistic approach to the issue. However, while the definition was expanded, it remained framed from a particular narrow perspective and one which does not explicitly address or link food to human and national security.

The United Nations (UN) Millennium Development Goals (MDG) and, in particular, MDG 1 designed to "eradicate extreme poverty and hunger", demonstrates the power and effectiveness of framing and emphasise a development perspective. The 2013 FAO report, which presents estimates of undernourishment and progress towards the MDG and WFS hunger targets shows that extreme hunger has been cut by half although one in eight people remain hungry. However, there have been setbacks caused by factors such as the global recession, high food and fuel prices, natural disasters, and conflicts. The FAO noted in its 2013 report that the recent vagaries of international food markets have moved vulnerability to food insecurity to the forefront of the food policy debate.

Within the international context of the UN, food has been framed from a development perspective. Its focus is on international development and the challenges associated with political and economic change in the international system to address global poverty and inequality, and the impact of globalisation on different parts of the world. The problems associated with this set of issues are compounded by challenges which have shaped the contemporary world, including the relationships between the global North and South, past colonialism activities, and capitalisms.

## Food insecurity

Food availability plays a prominent role in food security. Therefore it is imperative to take account of factors which might contribute to food security or lead to its insecurity. The follow sections will examine some of the issues which contribute to food insecurity, such as poverty, population, economic and physical access to food, ageing agricultural workers, land use and urbanisation

The FAO notes that policies aimed at enhancing agricultural productivity and increasing food availability, especially when smallholders are targeted, can achieve hunger reduction even where poverty is widespread. When these factors are combined with social protection and other measures that increase the incomes of poor families to buy food, they can have an even more positive effective and stimulate rural development, by creating markets and employment opportunities. In turn these can lead to equitable economic growth.

While supplying sufficient food to any given population is a necessity, it is not a condition to ensure that all people have adequate *access* to food. Food supplies over the past two decades have grown faster that the populations in developing countries and this has resulted in increased food availability for individuals and improved quality of diets through an increased range of food types. While this has generally contributed to an increase of 20 per cent in protein availability per person, diets in a number of African and Southern Asian nationstates have not improved. This lack of access, in some instances, has contributed to civil conflict. Economic access and physical access are pivotal issues associated with access to food.

Economic access is determined by disposable income, food prices and the provision of, and access to, social support. Improvements in economic access to food can be reflected by reduction in poverty rates. As noted by the FAO in its 2013 report, poverty and undernourishment have both declined over the past 20 years, albeit at different rates. Between 1990 and 2010, undernourishment rates reduced from 24 per cent to 15 per cent in developing regions as a whole, while poverty rates fell from 47 per cent to 24 per cent in 2008. Again as noted by the FAO, economic access is determined by people's purchasing power. The domestic food price index, defined as the ratio of food purchasing power parity (PPP) to general PPP, captures the cost of food relative to total consumption. The ratio has been on an increasing trend since 2001, but is now found to be at levels consistent with longer-term trends for most regions.

Physical access is the second key issue associated with access to food and can easily be disrupted by deliberate acts such as terrorism or conflict, or through the effects of natural disasters such as floods, droughts, hurricanes, earthquakes and fires. To a large extent, physical access is determined by the availability and quality of infrastructure, including ports, roads, railways, communication, food storage facilities and other installations that facilitate the functioning of markets. Incomes earned in agriculture, forests, fisheries and aquaculture play a primary role in determining food security outcomes. These issues affect overall economic and political stability and these have a direct impact on broader aspects of human security and that of individual nationstates.

## Food and security

The traditional security paradigm focuses on military threats to sovereign states. Yet the absence of war does not equal peace, security and stability. Security from the realist perspective, which Wæver describes as 'where states threaten each other, challenge each other's sovereignty, try to impose their will on each other, defend their independence, and so on', was the generally accepted paradigm. However, Halliday's description of the changing nature of security since the end of the Cold War characterises the shift in focus from military power (which was epitomised by the tension between the major actors in the Cold War) to a broadened security agenda. Unregulated population migration, human security, infectious diseases, food security, the environment, and terrorism are recognised as being part of it while also retaining aspects of the more traditional security characteristics such as war, inequality, and the importance of the state.

As noted previously, although food has not generally been associated with the traditional concept of security, there are examples throughout history where it has been used to leverage security and used as a weapon in war. Battles and wars have been lost or won on the basis of food supply and availability. For example, in 1648, the Siege of Candia, now called Heraklion in Crete was one of the longest sieges in history. After the Knights Hospitaller attacked an Ottoman convoy in 1644, the Turks responded by sending 60,000 men to assault Candia, which was controlled by the Knights' allies in Venice. Food and other supplies were prevented from entering the settlement for a considerable period of time. During Napoleon's era, the distance his armies could travel was inhibited by the availability and supply of food for the troops. However, Nicolas Appert discovered a way to contain food in a way which prevented it from spoiling. As a result, Napoleon's troops were able to advance further and he was able to feed his army at greater distances from food sources.

Last century, the siege of Leningrad in 1943 during World War II is a more recent notable example of the link between food and security, and as a tool of war. Both German and Finnish forces had the goal of encircling Leningrad and maintaining the blockade perimeter. The intention was to use food as a weapon against the people of Leningrad by cutting off all communication with the city and preventing the population from receiving any food or other supplies. Germany planned to use food as its key weapon against the citizens of Leningrad, and German scientists had calculated that the city would reach starvation after only a few weeks. According to a directive sent to Army Group North on 29 September, "After the defeat of Soviet Russia there can be no interest in the continued existence of this large urban center. ... Following the city's encirclement, requests for surrender negotiations shall be denied, since the problem of relocating and feeding the population cannot and should not be solved by us. In this war for our very existence, we can have no interest in maintaining even a part of this very large urban population" (Reid 2011: 135). The three million inhabitants of Leningrad had been caught unprepared and lacked sufficient supplies for a prolonged siege. The population experienced extreme hunger, freezing temperatures and disease as well as daily bombardments by the Luftwaffe. The siege and lack of food supplies lasted 872 days, and an estimated 1 million people, mostly civilians, died.

The 1974 Kissinger Report is another example where food had been linked to the security of a nationstate and considered as a potential leverage tool. This highly controversial document made reference to using food as a means to assist population reduction programs in targeted nationstates. The basic rationale of the report was that population growth in the least developed countries was a concern to US national security because it had the potential to lead to civil unrest and political instability in nationstates that had a high potential for economic development.

Notwithstanding the controversial nature of the report, the link between population and food is relevant to regional and global security as well as the stability of individual nationstates. There is an inexorable link in the food-population-climate-environment relationship which in turn directly affects food security. The current world population of around 7.2 billion is expected to increase by almost one billion in the next 12 years and reach between 8.3 and 10.4 billion by 2045. Estimates of how many people the planet can feed vary widely dependent on, among others, assumptions about land and water resources, diet, income and wealth distribution, nonetheless there appears to be an underlying assumption that when natural limits are reached, disaster will follow. As noted by Smil, determination of food energy needs at a population level is an extraordinarily complex challenge particularly because of the enormous variation in requirements and because of the capacity of humans to adapt to lower food availability.

As a result of the way the concept of security has been broadened and deepened, there has been a discernible shift from a period when it was inconceivable that food should be considered as a security issue and hold comparable status to economic, trade, or military issues. However, today global leaders and policy makers recognise that food has the potential to be a nontraditional challenge to the security not only of the nationstate but also to civil society and to individuals because if it is not addressed it can increase *in*security. Food and its security is an issue which needs to be taken seriously to meet the needs of the world's population in the twenty-first century when it is estimated that the population will reach up to 10.4 billion by 2045 and hold significant implications for global and regional security.

## Food regulations and security

Another issue which impacts food, its security and that of the wider population relates to regulatory failure. In an interdependent world trading system, regulatory failure in one country can impact many others, resulting in adverse public health repercussions in those countries. Appropriate and effective food regulations are relevant to developed as well as developing nationstates. Food safety laws and whether they are enforced is a critical factor and can hold significant trade and economic implications which in turn affect the security of a nationstate.

In the past few years, China has experienced a number of food safety incidents which resulted in consumer fear about food consumption. In response, China has taken a series of actions, such as food safety action, special renovation for food safety, and construction of a food safety credit system etc. For example, the 2008 melamine-tainted milk scandal in China 2008, generated a number of responses such as the replacement of the outdated Food Hygiene Act with the Food Safety Law, which came into effect in 2009. That law included provisions on risk assessment methods, establishment of a food safety committee, mandatory product recall requirements, and unification of food safety standards. China continues to address food safety issues and, in April 2014, it announced new food safety laws. Under the new laws, firms will be banned from operating if caught producing or selling unsafe foods. As a result of these new laws, if a company's food license is revoked, company executives and employees will not be allowed to work in the food industry for five years. However, some problems of producing and selling fake goods and other illegal activities are still very common.

## Food trade and economic implications for security

Food trade and economic implications are significant for the security and wellbeing of a nationstate and an issue which can affect food security is whether a nationstate is a net importer or exporter of food. The capacity of a nationstate to produce sufficient food to meet the needs of its civil society is subject to environmental conditions such as soil quality, access to water, agricultural productivity, production skills and infrastructure. 131 nations around the globe are net food importers.

China and Australia exemplify the different challenges faced by nationstates that are net importers and exporters of food. As a result of sustained economic growth in the past three decades, China has experienced a continued increase in consumer income, and this has led to significant changes in food consumption. Notwithstanding that

China is the world's largest producer, consumer, and trader of food, it is constrained by limited and degrading agricultural resources. As a result, China has been challenged by its inability to meet the changing and increasing demand from domestic production. This has led to concern that its domestic supply will not be able to meet the rising demand for food in the future. By comparison, Australian farmers produce almost 93 per cent of Australia's daily domestic food supply, and Australia is a net global food exporter. While China is a net importer of food to meet its consumer demand, Australia is a major food exporter of both processed and unprocessed food. Australia exports 60 per cent (in volume) of its total agricultural production with 14 per cent exported to China in 2012, with other major export markets being Japan (13 per cent), ASEAN (21 per cent), other Asia (16 per cent), European Union (eight per cent), Middle East (eight per cent), United States (seven per cent), and other nationstates (17 per cent).

China's domestic demand and consumption levels reflect the diversity of its changing civil society, particularly the differences in income levels notably between urban and rural communities. China's civil society attitudes, preferences and tastes towards food have changed and this is reflected in the higher demand for food, demand for a more diverse range of foods, demand for higher quality food, and the growth of away from home food consumption. Major factors identified by Zhou et al. which are driving these trends relate to rising real income, rapid urbanisation, changes in lifestyle, availability of new cooking methods, better organisation of food production and marketing, and changes in population structure. All these factors will continue to drive consumption higher, with the impact of urbanisation becoming even stronger. Among these factors, growth in income and urbanisation are the key drivers.

By comparison, although a net exporter of food, Australia faces a different particular set of challenges including issues associated with climate change, genetically modified organisms (GMOs), salinity, labour shortages, drought, trade access, pest control and water and native vegetation management, to name a few. These issues challenge Australia's capacity to continue to meet its domestic food demands and retain its position as one of the world's leading food exporters with consequent economic stability contributing to its national security.

There has been a high degree of re-structuring in Australian agricultural production since the mid-1980s. For example, during this period, grains have become even more export oriented, and there has been a shift to a more knowledge intense sector with an increasing, but unmet, demand for tertiary qualified graduates. Tertiary enrolments in agriculture science have been in decline since the mid1990s. Estimates indicate a potential demand for 6000 tertiary qualified graduates per year in the sector. However, the sector reportedly faces a significant undersupply of graduates, with Australian universities graduating fewer than 800 graduates per year in agriculture. This can be contrasted with China which produces more than 100,000 agriculture graduates a year. The shift to a more knowledge intense sector has long term implications for productivity capacity, the economy and trade.

## Ageing population

Australia also faces a declining and ageing agricultural population. The median age of farmers in 2006 was fifty-two years, much higher than the median age of 40 years in all other occupations and reflects the problems of "greying farmers". In 2012, the median farm age was fifty-three, by far the oldest of any economic sector. However, this issue is not restricted to Australia and it is one which has been developing globally for some years. Farmers, generally, are older that the population at large in a number of nationstates. For example, the proportion of farmers over age sixty-five in the United States, Canada, Japan and South Korea is much higher than the proportion of the total population over sixty-five years of age. In 1998 in the United States, it was reported that the average age of the general labour force was thirty-eight, while that of fulltime farmers was fifty-seven. In 2012, it was reported that the average age of farmers in the US was fifty-eight years, sixty-seven years in Japan, and more than one third of European farmers were older than sixty-five, while in China the average was around sixty. While the age of farmers is not generally considered to be a factor associated directly with food security, it does affect a nationstate's capacity to meet the needs of its own population as well as affect its trade and economic capacity. In turn, this can have implications for its overall security.

## Conflict

Conflict can directly affect food security whether the conflict is in the form of communal violence, protest and rioting, civil conflict or interstate war. When food production, its supply, and distribution are at risk or threatened either through deliberate actions or natural hazards, there can be significant wider implications. Food insecurity is neither a necessary nor a sufficient condition for violent conflict although the two are often linked. If a nationstate is unable to meet the food consumption needs of its civil society then it risks internal conflict and political instability.

## Land use

Changes to land use can be a source of conflict and increased urbanisation can reduce the amount of arable land. With 70 per cent of the global population likely to live in cities by 2045, urbanisation will be a particularly important theme in developing countries. Urbanisation is likely to enhance economic and social development, and may lead to pressure on the environment and land use which could contribute to social tensions within the urban population.

China has 22 per cent of the world's population, but less than 10 per cent of its arable land. In China the majority of the available arable land is used for producing food. For example, in 2010, the total area sown to all crops in the nation was 161 m ha. Of this, 96 per cent was devoted to food production. However, increased urbanisation presents challenges to China's production ability. Any future increase in total food output can be achieved only through yield improvement or claiming new land for crops. Increased urbanisation tends to influence and change dietary behaviours and urbanisation affects not only the consumption level of different foods, but also the composition of what food is consumed.

The situation is further complicated by the quality of arable land. According to a national soil quality report in April 2014 produced by the Ministry of Environment Protection of the People's Republic of China, almost one-fifth of China's arable land is polluted to various degrees. The report, based on seven-years' worth of tests on 6.3 million square kilometres of land, also found that 16 per cent of the country's soil is contaminated, with one per cent heavily polluted. This has both long term implications for China's capacity to meet its food requirements and it has the potential to impact its food export capacity. For example, in the past, the US-China relationship has been based primarily on economic interests, however, contaminated soil and potentially export crop production would shift the focus away from economic interests to a public health one.

Australia, as the world's ninth largest agriculture producer, is one of the most foodsecure nations in the world although it has only just over six per cent of arable land (includes about 27 million hectares of cultivated grassland). According to the Australian Bureau of Agricultural and Resource Economics, Australia's terrestrial and aquatic food producers are capable of producing enough food to feed approximately 80 million people per year. Measured by people per square kilometre of arable land, Australia has 68 times more than Japan, 25 times more than the United Kingdom, 22 times more than China and four times more than the United States. However, according to statistics kept by the FAO, there has been a consistent trend of diminishing agricultural land in Australia since 1976. At that time, nearly 490 million hectares was either arable land, dedicated to permanent crops or suitable for grazing. Over the subsequent 33 years, that area diminished by more than 16 per cent while Australia's population increased from 13 million to one of 22 million. Approximately half of the loss of agricultural land occurred between 2005 and 2009. Australia lost 36 million hectares of agricultural land in that short period of time. Australia also faces a long-term trend of a growing urbanised population, and there has been an ongoing practice to protect natural environments. These combined factors will lead to agricultural land becoming a diminishing resourcc that is more intensively farmed as its area shrinks.

## Communal violence

Communal conflict, that is organised violence between non-state groups mobilised along a shared communal identity, is often a result of competition over scarce resources, particularly arable land and water. For example, in March 2014 there were communal riots in Myanmar due to shortages of food, drinking water and medical care. Such conflict can also escalate to involve government forces such as in Darfur and Burundi, and escalate further into civil war if the government is perceived to support or favour one group over another.

**Protests and riots**

Protests and riots throughout history have often been linked to high food prices or sudden breaks in food supply and distribution, whether intentional or caused through natural events. For example, following the impact of Hurricane Katrina in the US in 2005, looters rapidly depleted stores of shelves of food among many other items.

As noted earlier, record high food prices in 2008 caused rioting and violence in 48 countries. Van Baun has noted that the ratio of violent to nonviolent protest was higher in low income countries and in countries with lower government effectiveness. Since the early 1980s, many fragile countries have experienced recurrent fiscal crises that have severely curtailed their ability to intervene in domestic markets and ensure food security. Such structural weaknesses are exacerbated during conflicts and can lead to higher food prices. In turn this can intensify conflicts.

Changes in government subsidies can also be a source of conflict and rioting. For example, in 1977 the Egyptian government removed state subsidies for basic foodstuffs as mandated by the International Monetary Fund. This resulted in what was described as 'the three-day bread-riots' in which over 800 people died. In 2008, Egypt again experienced food riots. Egypt's problems were part of a global phenomenon, in that the price of the wheat it imported – half the country's needs – had tripled since the summer. The price rises highlighted the fragility of the ruling political regime and its weakening economy. Political opposition to the government was divided with the outlawed Muslim Brotherhood as the most powerful component of the opposition forces. The nexus between food and political stability directly impacted the security of the civilian population, and changes in agricultural and food polices can exacerbate already vulnerable nationstates.

## Civil conflict

Civil conflict is the prevalent type of armed conflict in the twenty-first century. There have been a total of 244 armed conflicts in 151 locations worldwide since the end of World War II to 2012. In 2009, there were 36 cases of armed conflict, one less than the previous year. However, this was substantially less than during the peak years of the 1990s during which over fifty conflicts were recorded annually. As noted by the FAO, civil conflict is almost exclusively a phenomenon of countries with low levels of economic development and high levels of food insecurity. According to the FAO, 65 per cent of the world's food-insecure people live in seven countries: India, China, the Democratic Republic of Congo (DRC), Bangladesh, Indonesia, Pakistan and Ethiopia. With the exception of China, all of these nationstates have experienced civil conflict in the past decade, with DRC, Ethiopia, India and Pakistan recently embroiled in notable civil conflicts.

## Famine and population migration

While many countries worldwide face food security crises, with large numbers of people hungry and unable to find enough food, only rarely do the conditions meet the humanitarian community's formal criteria for a famine. According to the UN, a famine can be declared only when certain measures of mortality, malnutrition and hunger are met. Those conditions are: at least 20 per cent of households in an area face extreme food shortages with a limited ability to cope; acute malnutrition rates exceed 30 per cent; and the death rate exceeds two persons per day per 10,000 persons. While these criteria have been developed and applied, the declaration of a famine carries no binding obligations on the UN or Member States, but serves to focus global attention on the problem.

Often by the time a famine has been declared, large numbers of people have already begun to travel in search of food, arable land and water resources. Unregulated population flows are defined here as the forced, or unsanctioned (by governments) movement of people across borders and within states for economic reasons, or as a consequence of war, persecution or environmental factors. This definition is broader than the one used by the majority of studies on unregulated population movements which focus on people categorised as refugees by the United Nations under the 1951 Convention and its 1967 Protocol. However, the United Nation's definition is relatively restrictive as it significantly understates the number of people forced to move for reasons beyond their influence or control. The UN definition does not encompass people who move internally or across state borders for environmental and economic reasons.

In 1975, the overall number of refugees globally, as measured by the United Nations High Commissioner for Refugees (UNHCR), was around 2.4 million. However, by 1992, this figure had risen dramatically to 18.2 million. Yet, in 2014 the UNHCR announced there were 51.2 million forcibly displaced people at the end of 2013, a full six million higher than the previous year. The data covers three groups: refugees, asylum-seekers, and the internally displaced. Food related issues are often linked to those population groups.

In July 2014 the UN announced that nearly 800,000 refugees in Africa have had their food rations cut due to a lack of global aid funding, threatening to push many to the brink of starvation. In a joint statement the United Nations' World Food Programme (WEF) and refugee agency UNHCR said the cuts of up to 60 per cent are "threatening to worsen already unacceptable levels of acute malnutrition, stunting and anaemia, particularly in children". The situation was described as most dire for the 300,000 refugees in Chad, mainly from Sudan's Darfur region and from the Central African Republic, whose rations had been cut by as much as 60 per cent. In many cases people were left with rations of just 850 calories per day, compared to the recommended 2,100 calories adults should receive to remain healthy. "Desperately hungry refugees continue to cross daily into southern Chad from the strife-torn Central African Republic, only to find that hunger does not stop at the border", the statement said. At the same time, UN agencies reported that supplies had also been cut by at least half for some 150,000 refugees in Central Africa and in South Sudan, while another 338,000 refugees in Liberia, Burkina Faso, Mozambique, Ghana, Mauritania and Uganda had seen their rations dwindle up to 43 per cent. Since early 2013, a series of unexpected, temporary ration reductions, sometimes due to insecurity, and political instability, had affected camps in several countries, including Kenya, Ethiopia, the Congo, the Democratic Republic of Congo and Cameroon.

These examples demonstrate the point that while food security is described by the WHO as existing when "all people at all times have access to sufficient, safe, nutritious food to maintain a healthy and active life", there are wider security implications for individuals as well as whole populations and individual nationstates and regions such as associated with human security, unregulated population migration and border tensions.

## Conclusion

The issues of food and its security affect all nationstates regardless of whether they are a net exporter or importer of food. It is evident that some nationstates and their civil societies are more vulnerable and hence more insecure regarding the availability of, and access to, appropriate quality food. When looked at in a holistic way from a systems perspective it is apparent that the link between food and the effects of environmental and climatic conditions, as well as actions by non-state actors can impact market volatility, political instability and human security.

This chapter has demonstrated that while the WHO definition of food security offers a useful tool and set of parameters, there are other equally important considerations which should be taken into account. The effects of conflict can increase food insecurity and, conversely, food insecurity can increase conflict and contribute to political insecurity and undermine the security of a nationstate and its civil society.

# References


Agricultural Market Information System, (2014), 'AMIS Crops', at http://www.amis-outlook.org/amis-about/amis-crops/crops-rice/en

ABARES, (2012), 'Australian Commodities', December Quarter 2011, Canberra, ABARES.

Australian Bureau of Statistics, (2010), *Australian Social Trends, March 2009*, Catalogue No. 4102.0, Canberra. ABS.

Australia Bureau of Statistics, (2012), 'Labour Force and other characteristics of Farmers' Feature Article in *1301.0 – Year Book Australia*, Canberra, ABS at http://www.abs.gov.au/-ausstats/abs@.nsf/Lookup/by%20Subject/1301.0-2012-Main%20Features-Home%20page1.

BBC News, (2000), 'Flashback 1984: Portrait of a Famine', at http://news.bbc.co.uk/2/hi/africa/703958.stm.

Dupont, A., (1997), 'Unregulated population flows in East Asia: A new security', *Pacifica Review: Peace, Security & Global Change, formerly Pacifica Review: Peace, Security & Global Change*, Vol 9, No 1, pp 1-22.

FAO (1996) 'Declaration on World Food Security', World Food Summit, Geneva, FAO.

FAO, (2003), Food Security: Concepts and Measurement', in *Trade Reforms and Food Security: Conceptualizing the Linkages* (FAO: Economic and Social Development Department, 2003), Geneva, FAO.

FAO, (2010). 'FAOSTAT Database'. Geneva, FAO at http://faostat.fao.org /

FAO, (2013) *The State of Food Insecurity in the World*, Geneva, FAO.

Feltz, L. (2012), 'Political Globalization and Civil War in Former British Colonies', in *The Cupola*, Gettysburg, Paper 12.

Flynn, D. (2013) 'Letter From the Editor: Our Stake in China's Food Safety', in *Food Safety News*, at http://www.foodsafetynews.com/2013/09/letter-from-the-editor-our-stake-in-chinas-food-safety/#.UknWDxbMGEk.

Fu, J, (2009), 'The 2008 China Milk Scandal and the Role of the Government in Corporate Governance in China', Conference paper, at http://www.clta.edu.au/professional/papers-/conference2009/FuCLTA09.pdf .

Guangxing, S., Tian, T, (2012), 'Study on China's Food Safety Issues and Supervision Platform Based on Credit Management', ICPM-2012, in *Crisis Management in the Time of Changing World*, Paris, Atlantis Press, at www.atlantis-press.com/php/download_paper.-php?id=2911.

Halliday, F., (1991), 'International Relations: Is There a New Agenda?', in *Millennium – Journal of International Studies*, Vol 20, No 57, pp. 57-72.

Harbom, L.; Wallensteen, P. (2010). Armed Conflicts, 1946-2009. *Journal of Peace Research*, Vol 47, Issue 4, pp. 501-509.

Huang, J. and Rozelle, S. (1998), 'Market Development and Food Demand in Rural China', *China Economic Review*, Vol. 9, pp. 25-45, at http://www.mep.gov.cn/gkml/hbb-/qt/201404/t20140417_270670.htm.

Johansson, E, ( 2011), 'Managing Communal Conflicts: The Role of the State', Conference Paper presented at the 52nd Annual Convention of the International Studies Association Montreal, Canada, 16-19 March 2011, at https://www.academia.edu/720046/Emma-_Johansson_Managing_Communal_Conflicts_The_Role_of_the_State_

Jöhr, H. (2012) 'Where are the Future Farmers to Grow Our Food?', in *International Food and Agribusiness Management Review*, Volume 15, Special Issue A.

Judah, A., (2011), 'No Shortage of Land or Food ... or Hot Air', The Drum, ABC online, 1 July 2011, at http://www.abc.net.au/news/2011-07-01/judah3a/2778510.

Kahl, C., (2006), *States, Scarcity, and Civil Strife in the Developing World*. Princeton, Princeton University Press.

Kissinger, H, (1974), *National Security Study Memorandum 200: Implications of Worldwide Population Growth for US Security and Overseas*, (NSSM 200) Washington DC, at http://nixon.archives.gov/virtuallibrary/documents/nssm/nssm_200.pdf.

'Land Use', in *The World Factbook*, at https://www.cia.gov/library/publications/the-world-factbook/fields/2097.html.

McIntyre, L., (2013) 'Policy Framing of Household Food Insecurity in Canada: Why getting the problem wrong leads to faulty solutions', PowerPoint presentation, at http://www.centrelearoback.org/assets/PDF/CLR-GCPB131212_McIntyre_PresEn.pdf .

Millbank, A., (1994) *Global Population Movements, Temporary Movements in the Asia-Pacific Region and Australia's Immigration Program*, Research Paper no. 13, Canberra, Parliament of Australia.

Ministry of Defence, (2014), *Strategic Trends Programme Global Strategic Trends – Out to 2045*, Fifth edition, London.

Mitleton-Kelly, E., (2003), 'Ten Principles of Complexity and Enabling Infrastructures', in MitletonKelly, E. (ed) *Complex Systems and Evolutionary Perspectives on Organisations: The Application of Complexity Theory to Organisations*, Oxford, Elsevier Science Ltd., pp. 23-50.

Moncrief, M, (2012), 'Agricultural Land Diminishing, Statistics Show', in *The Age* newspaper, at http://www.theage.com.au/national/agricultural-land-diminishing-statistics-show-20120525-1za05.html#ixzz36NKylQIj.

National Farmers Federation, (2012), *NFF Farm Facts 2012*, at http://www.nff.org.au/farm-facts.html.

Office of the Chief Scientist, *Health of Australia Science*, Commonwealth of Australia, Canberra, section 4.7.

Page, H., (2013) *Global Governance and Food Security as Global Public Good*, Center on International Cooperation, New York, New York University, August 2013.

PMSEIC (2010). *Australia and Food Security in a Changing World.* Canberra, The Prime Minister's Science, Engineering and Innovation Council.

Pratley J. E.; Hay, M. (2010), *The Job Market in Agriculture in Australia.* Wagga Wagga, Australian Council of Deans of Agriculture.

Productivity Commission, (2005), 'Trends in Australia Agriculture', Commission Research Paper, Canberra, at http://www.pc.gov.au/research/commission/agriculture

Reid, A. (2011), *Leningrad: The Epic Siege of World War II, 1941–1944.* New York, Walker and Co., at pp 134-135.

Smil, V., (1994), 'How Many People Can the Earth Feed', *Population and Development Review*, Vol 20, No, 2, pp. 255-292.

Smith, M.Y., Stacey, R.,(1997), 'Governance and Cooperative Networks: An Adaptive Systems Perspective', in *Technological Forecasting and Social Change*, Vol 54, No 1, pp 79-94.

Stinger, R., (2000), 'Food Security in Developing Countries', *CIES Discussion Paper 0011*, Adelaide, University of Adelaide.

UNHCR, (2014) 'Global Refugee Numbers Highest Since World War Two', media release 24 June 2014, Geneva UNHCR, at http://www.newvision.co.ug/news/656896-global-refugee-numbers-highest-since-wwii-un.html

UNHCR, (2014) 'As food shortages hit 800,000 African refugees, UNHCR and WFP issue urgent appeal', media release 1 July 2014, Geneva UNHCR, at http://www.unhcr.org/53b2a1969.html.

UN News Centre, 'When Food Security Becomes a Famine', at http://www.un.org/apps/news/story.asp?NewsID=39113

United States Department of Agriculture, *United States Census of Agriculture, 1969 and 1997*, USDA Census of Agriculture Historical Archive, Cornell University, Ithaca, NY.

Von Braun, J, (2008), *The World Food Crisis: Political and Economic Consequences and Needed Actions*, Presentation to the Ministry of Foreign Affairs, Stockholm, Sweden, 22 September 2008, at http://www.slideshare.net/jvonbraun/the-world-food-crisis-political-and-economic-consequences-and-needed-actions.

Wæver, O., (2011), 'Securitization', in Hughes, C. W.; Meng, L.Y. (Editors), *Security Studies: A Reader*, London, Routledge.

Wang Y, 'Almost One-Fifth of China's Arable Land is Polluted', in *China Dialogue* 24 April 2014, at http://www.chinafile.com/Almost-One-Fifth-Chinas-Arable-Land-Polluted.

Wibbles, E., (2006) 'Dependency Revisited: International Markets, Business Cycles and Social Spending in the Developing World', in *International Organization*, Vol 60, Issue, 2, pp. 433-369.

Wilmoth, J.R., Ball, P., (1992), 'The Population Debate in American Popular Magazines', in *Population and Development Review*, Vol 18, No 4, pp. 631-68.

World Health Organization, 'Food Security', at http://www.who.int/trade/glossary/story028/en/

Zhou, Z., Tian, W., Wang, J., Liu, H., Cao, L., (2012), *Food Consumption Trends in China 2012 Report*, Canberra, Department of Agriculture and Fisheries.

# 7

# Competitiveness of food processing clusters in Australia and China

John Dalrymple

## Introduction

The food processing sector of many developed and developing economies is dominated by small and medium-sized enterprises (SME). For example, the food industry in the European Union is one of the largest employers (Avermaete, Viaene, Morgan, Pitts, Crawford, and Mahon 2004), the Toronto food cluster (Donald and Blay-Palmer 2006), Malaysia (Saleh and Ndubisi 2006) and developing countries (Ceglie, Clara and Dini 1999; Arbor and Coenen 2005; Wilkinson 2008). In countries where there has been significant migration, such firms make a substantial contribution to the local economy and frequently develop and grow from being purely local providers to become national providers, link with major companies and become suppliers (Gellynck, Vermeireand and Viaene 2007; Blundel and Hingley 2001) and, in some cases, exporters (Requier-Desjardins, Boucher and Cerdan 2003). The creation of jobs and a vibrant food processing sector can invigorate rural areas as the technology to retain nutritional value of processed food removes the potential losses from long distance transport of fresh and processed produce (North and Smallbone 2000).

The food production and processing industries were traditionally relatively insulated from global competition by the perishability of produce and the relatively high logistics and distribution costs associated with shipping and haulage of relatively low value goods (Traill 1997). However, the emergence of the power of large supermarket chains and the streamlining of transportation through containerisation and container refrigeration has reduced the influence of these non-tariff barriers. This has provided an imperative for food processing SME sector firms to improve their competitiveness.

Competitiveness has been assisted by the development of clusters of firms and these have been studied in a number of jurisdictions (Robertson and Patel 2007; Donald and Blay-Palmer 2006; Requier-Desjardins, Boucher and Cerdan 2003). It has been recognised that clustering of firms has resulted in significant innovation in the cluster industry sector (North and Smallbone 2000; Blay-Palmer and Donald 2006; Bertolini and Giovannetti 2006; Johnston 2004). Clusters have also been viewed as an approach to sustained economic development (North and Smallbone 2000; Asheim, and Coenen, 2005; Karaev, Koh and Szamosi 2007). The link between primary production and the clustering of food processors has also resulted in the integration of food processing supply chains (Blundel and Hingley 2001). Variety in the countries of origin of the cuisines has added further vibrancy to the food industry clusters in a number of countries (Blay-Palmer and Donald 2006). Whilst Australia has a long history of indigenous inhabitants, the country has, today, a very diverse population from numerous countries of origin as a result of migration.

Furthermore, there are many countries where there have been waves of migration, for example, Canada, United States of America,

Mauritius, New Zealand, Australia, the UK, and France. In all cases, the migration process has impacted on the local food consumption and the associated processing industries. This has frequently involved significant innovation in the food processing industry companies through the adoption and adaption of elements of the foods of other countries. Innovation has been in the form of both ingredients and processing methods resulting in fusion cuisine (Blay-Palmer and Donald 2006). This chapter presents the experience of the development of a food processing industry cluster in Melbourne's North, its contribution to the economic activity of the region and the increasing necessity to remain competitive in a globalised economy. There are many similarities between the settlement patterns in Australia, where migration has been concentrated in the coastal cities where migrant labour moved into low skilled manufacturing jobs and the internal migration patterns over the past few decades in China (Chan 2008). There has been significant internal migration from the provinces with agrarian economies to the coastal and other major cities where the 'factories of the world' are located. Many of the migrants resettled very long distances from their province of origin and the provincial cuisine was therefore translated to their new locations (Chan 2008). The development of food processing industry clusters in Melbourne's North and their quest for improved competitiveness may provide leading indicators for the developing industries in China.

## Migration patterns in Melbourne Australia

The migration of people to Australia has been evident since European settlement. However, the most concentrated and widespread migration has taken place since World War II. In the immediate aftermath of that war, the Australian government entered into a series of formal and informal agreements with a variety of European countries to enable migration of citizens of those countries to Australia. The migration agreements included Mediterranean countries Italy and Greece as well as Turkey, Yugoslavia, Germany and Austria. Further significant migration from Hungary (post 1956), Czechoslovakia (post 1968), Chile (post 1973), Indochina (post 1975) and Poland (post 1981) took place to accommodate refugees from political upheaval in these countries. The overall effect on the demographics of Australia has been that between the end of World War II and the Census of 2011, the population had risen from seven million, with 90 per cent born in Australia, to over 22 million, with over 25 per cent born overseas (DIBP 2014).

In the case of Greater Melbourne, the waves of migration followed the pattern of the Australian migration, broadly speaking and, in the 2011 Census, a number of the local government areas in the region had one third or more of the population who were born overseas. There are substantial representations of people of Italian, Greek, Macedonian, Vietnamese, Chinese, Indian and Sri Lankan origins in the region, with many other ethnic origins represented ABS (2014).

## The development of the food processing industry in Melbourne's north

As migrants travelled to, and settled in, Australia, they wished to continue to consume food that was familiar to them. The entrepreneurial migrants identified opportunities both in the restaurant sector and in the grocery and supply sector. Initially these businesses were located where there were concentrations of the ethnic minority from which the supplier came. With increased migration, there was a necessity to provide housing, schools and other infrastructure and establish new suburbs and new communities as the city grew. Some of the migrants remained in the communities where they were first accommodated, while others moved to the new communities that were being created. Consequently, some established businesses moved to the new communities, while others remained. This, in turn, enabled the development of communities where residents who came from many different ethnic backgrounds became aware of, and accessed, both fresh and processed foods from different local ethnic groupings.

The development of innovation in the food sector then arose from the growth of communities from different ethnic origins consuming food and produce that were previously unknown to them. In many cases, the food would be adopted or adapted by the restaurateurs or the food suppliers to match the taste requirements and demands of these new markets. In the first instance, many of the food items were imported from the country of origin. However, as many of the migrants had their origins in agrarian environments, these people had the knowledge and skills to engage in food processing. For example, the production of cheese and other dairy products, the production of sauces and cold cuts, smoked and other preserved foods were all part of life in an agrarian community. In many countries the harvest was followed by some form of preservation of food and produce to maintain sufficient food stocks to provide year round supply. This market demand for food that was available by importation, coupled with the knowledge and ability to access local supplies and use the local ingredients to provide acceptable substitutes, resulted in entrepreneurs engaging in import substitution. This substitution provided foodstuffs that were fresher and tailored to the needs of the local market and did not require to be transported from, for example, Europe. This development, in turn, enabled regular stock replenishment and lower costs for the restaurateurs and the proprietors of food and produce shopkeepers and merchants. The development of primary production and food processing made a significant contribution to the economic development of the region.

## The contribution of the food processing industry to the economy in Melbourne's North

The food processing industry in Melbourne's North began as a disparate set of businesses. The businesses predominantly represent the cuisines from the major countries of origin of the migrants of the last century. The location of the business was originally based on proximity to the family home, since most began as small, family run, businesses. Some cheese and dairy product producers located their production facility in farm buildings, while others moved into factory premises. These businesses provided direct employment for production workers, but also required products and services to support their business operations. This resulted in the development of, for example, a food industry machinery manufacturing sector that could design and install high quality plant and equipment that was suitable for production of food in an environment that satisfied the highest standards of food safety. This usually involved the design and fabrication of plant and equipment in stainless steel, providing highly skilled jobs in the region. The development of the food cluster in Melbourne's north attracted the attention of both State and local government.

The local authorities in the region recognised the existence of a vibrant 'food manufacturing cluster' in Melbourne's North incorporating meat processing, dairy processing, sauces, herbs and spices, fruit and vegetables, specialty baked products, packaged products (canned, bottled, bagged, etc) and identified the need to quantify the extent of the cluster and its contribution to the employment and economic wellbeing of the region. A snapshot of the companies in the region was sought by the local authorities and, as a result, a sample of twelve companies in the region was selected to establish an estimate of the economic activity. The aggregate data are presented in Table 7.1.

**Table 7.1 – Aggregate data for the sample companies**

| Company Data | |
|---|---|
| Number of employees | 715 |
| Total annual cost of materials used in process (ingredients) (Au$) | 116214690 |
| Inventory Value at Last Valuation (Au$) | 6343656 |
| Number of Delivery Vehicles Owned by Firms | 12 |
| Total Floor Area (Square m) | 16320 |
| Warehousing Floor Area (Square m) | 5336 |
| Company turnover in last financial year | 220549457 |
| Number of orders in last financial year | 316691 |

The twelve companies employed 715 people in the region and procured over Au$116 million worth of ingredients and carried over Au$6 million in inventory at most recent valuation. This produced an annual total turnover of over Au$220 million as a result of filling over 300 thousand orders. The firms only owned twelve delivery vehicles, so it could be inferred that there was a significant flow on of logistics and distribution activity that created employment and further economic activity.

The modern food processing industry also required a number of services in addition to the usual suite of professional services required by businesses. For example, third party certification of their processes to ISO 9000 and a Hazard Analysis and Critical Control Points (HACCP) based control system to assure food safety. The local government organisations were also interested in the multiplier effect on employment and economic activity of the food processors in their region, since that represented the resource base for local government taxation as well as improving the employment rates among the citizens of the region, underpinning the economic wellbeing of the region. The average company data for the sample is presented in Table 7.2.

**Table 7.2 – Average data for the sample companies**

| Company Data | |
|---|---|
| Number of employees | 60 |
| Total cost of materials used in process (ingredients)(Au$) | 9684558 |
| Inventory Value at Last Valuation (Au$) | 528638 |
| Number of Delivery Vehicles Owned by Firms | 1 |
| Total Floor Area (Square m) | 1360 |
| Warehousing Floor Area (Square m) | 445 |
| Company turnover in previous financial year (Au$) | 18379121 |
| Number of orders in the previous financial year | 26391 |

Table 7.3 provides an indication of the range of size of companies in the sample. The companies range from four to two hundred and eighty employees and turnover ranged from a quarter of a million dollars to one hundred million dollars. There are also a number of medium range companies in the sample as indicated by the average values for turnover, etc.

**Table 7.3 – Minimum and maximum data for the sample companies**

| Company Data | Min | Max |
|---|---|---|
| Number of employees | 4 | 280 |
| Total cost of materials used in process (ingredients) ($) | 100000 | 62,400,000 |
| Inventory Value at Last Valuation ($) | 120000 | 8933000 |
| Number of Delivery Vehicles Owned by Firm | 0 | 9 |
| Total Floor Area (Square m) | 300 | 7494 |
| Warehousing Floor Area (Square m) | 100 | 1500 |
| Company turnover in last financial year | 250000 | 100,000,000 |
| Number of orders in last financial year | 94 | 240000 |

From the data presented for the sample companies, it is quite clear that the food processing sector represented a substantial element of the economic activity of the region. At the time of this research project, the sample represented approximately 10 per cent of the companies in the regional food processing cluster of companies.

## The food processing industry supply chain

One of the major interests of the local government was to quantify the impact of the presence of the food industry cluster on the economic wellbeing of the region. This depended on the amount of the firms' expenditures that flowed through to the local economy through purchasing from local suppliers. Data collection provided numerical values for ingredients, expenditure on supplies to support administrative processes, packaging supplies, capital plant and equipment, warehousing and distribution, infrastructure, systems support services, business services, and other services. The location of the vendor of goods and services was also part of the data set. The results were as follows:

## Ingredients

For all companies, the ingredients constituted a substantial cost component, ranging between 30 per cent and 73 per cent of company turnover. Despite the attraction of mapping the supply chain for ingredients, the main ingredients for the sample companies were commodities like meat, milk, flour, fruit, vegetables, etc. As the output of primary producers the processors purchased from producers located close to the location of primary production. For example, meat and poultry were initially processed close to the farms producing the animals and poultry before being transported for further processing. In the case of milk and flour, ingredients were sourced from dairy processors and flour mills located close to the dairy farms and cereal growers respectively. The same was true of, for example, industries consuming significant quantities of sugar. Most other ingredients were sourced locally, either in Melbourne's North or other parts of Melbourne. Other than those ingredients mentioned, very few ingredients were sourced interstate and very few ingredients were imported from overseas by companies in the sample

### Administration processes

The sample companies spend was of the order of $335,000 on office equipment and supplies. It was notable that very little office equipment was leased constituting less than 10 per cent of the overall spend. All of these supplies were sourced either locally or in the Greater Melbourne area.

### Packaging materials

After ingredients, the next largest spend was on packaging supplies. The total spend was in excess of $2.5 million. Cardboard boxes, plastic containers, food grade film and labels were the most common purchases. Over 90 per cent of respondents indicated that they purchased their packaging materials either locally namely in the region or in Greater Melbourne.

### Plant and equipment

The purchase of plant and equipment is always a sporadic activity in SME sector firms, with capital expenditure often taking place at most every few years. A number of the sample companies reported zero capital spending for the period covered. The expenditure on plant and equipment and bought in maintenance for the sample was just under $1million, with capital investment making up 80 per cent and maintenance the remaining 20 per cent. Examination of the supply chain for plant and equipment indicated that companies sourced capital items locally, in Greater Melbourne, Victoria or elsewhere in Australia. Specialist equipment was imported. The maintenance of equipment was sourced locally, in Greater Melbourne and from elsewhere in Victoria.

### Warehousing and distribution

The total reported spending on warehousing and distribution was estimated to be over $1.5million. Two thirds of that was reported as cost of third party distribution. This was consistent with reported low levels of in-house delivery vehicle ownership. Clearly third party logistics and distribution had been embraced by those in the industry. There was very little reported expenditure on externally sourced warehousing. The remaining reported expenditures were on in-house distribution and in-house warehousing. Most of the companies in the sample distributed throughout Australia and some engaged in exporting and the sourcing of logistics and distribution reflected those requirements.

### Infrastructure

Expenditure on infrastructure items, like software packages and the implementation of other systems was, like capital expenditure, a sporadic activity and the total reported spend on all such systems was estimated to be the order of $100,000. A number of the companies reported no expenditure on additional software packages and systems implementation. Infrastructure expenditure was reported to be all in the Greater Melbourne area.

## Systems support services

The reported system support services expenditure was also comparatively low, estimated to be of the order of $100,000. A number of companies reported no expenditure and it may be that some of the larger companies provide first line support services in-house. Furthermore, there may be a crossover with expenditure on 'business services' where support may be sought in the form of 'consultancy', rather than as a routine ongoing support service. Those support services that were reported were sourced either locally or in the Greater Melbourne area.

## Business services

The estimated spend on business services was upwards of $300,000. The expenditures were mainly on consultancy and other advisory services, quality and other system certification services, with similar expenditures on accounting services, HR training and development and recruitment each had similar spends. Some of the larger companies will handle these matters in-house, or source services from another part of the organisation. These services were reported as being sourced from Greater Melbourne or from elsewhere in Australia.

## Other services

The expenditure on other services was estimated to be upwards of $200,000 with external laboratory testing and property maintenance dominating. Pest control, office cleaning and production area cleaning were the next similar sized grouping, with external calibration services being the only other significant expenditure. These services were sourced from Greater Melbourne or elsewhere in Victoria.

### Contribution to the region's economy

This sample was a self-selecting and may not have been representative of the cluster. However, it contained a mix of large, medium-sized and small enterprises and that was the pattern in the cluster as a whole. If this had been a truly representative sample, then the cluster represented a group of companies that employed over 7,000 people, turned over $2200 million with a turnover per employee and value added per employee that significantly exceeded corresponding measures for other traditional manufacturing sectors. These were important attributes from the perspective of retaining the jobs and economic activity in Melbourne's North. The supplier investigation indicated that the main expenditures were on 'raw materials' or ingredients and that most of these were sourced from locations relatively close to primary production. These included centres where there were, for example, abattoirs, flour mills, sugar refiners and major dairy complexes. From the perspective of animal welfare, locations of abattoirs continue to be concentrated in close proximity to primary producers. There had been rationalisation of the dairy industry, but that resulted in larger facilities relatively close to primary production. The reported expenditures in categories other than raw materials or ingredients indicated that much of the expenditure was localised in the region or Greater Metropolitan Melbourne. Food handling plant and equipment was manufactured in the catchment area of the cluster and many businesses took advantage of this proximity and purchased locally.

### Benchmarking food processors to improve competitiveness

Benchmarking can be a powerful tool to assist in the pursuit of improved competitiveness. There are two types of benchmarking, one is business profile benchmarking and the second is business process benchmarking. In business profile benchmarking, the aim is to compare a number of key indicators of company performance for companies that are similar in terms of number of employees, industry sector, and annual turnover. This comparison provides a profile of indicators of company performance against a peer comparison group. To preserve data anonymity, it is necessary to benchmark a group of at least ten similar companies. The profile presents the company's position in terms of the quartile that it lies in for each of the measures of performance. Where a company lies in the bottom quartile, it is important to examine whether this is a cause for concern, or if it is a function of the business and is, consequently, inevitable. Once business profile benchmarking has been carried out, it is possible for the firm to identify potential opportunities for improvement. The opportunities for improvement then enable the identification of processes that might be the subject of business process benchmarking so that the firm might benchmark their process against the same process of a company that is recognised as an exemplar in the field. In this case, it need not be a firm that is in the same industry sector, but a firm that is well known for their competitiveness in that particular process.

In the case of this food cluster, the key performance measures selected were: Value added per employee, Stock turn, Production space/Warehouse space, Warehouse space/Total space, Ingredients/Turnover, Turnover per employee, Average order value, Turnover per square metre, Turnover per square metre devoted to production.

Turnover per employee and value added per employee are measures of productivity. Production space/Warehouse space, Warehouse space/Total space, Turnover per square metre, Turnover per square metre devoted to production are measures of the effectiveness of use of expensive factory space. Ingredients/Turnover indicates the cost base of the company. Stock turn is a measure of how well the company manages its working capital. Average order value is a measure of the proportion of turnover devoted to the administration, picking, packing and delivery of orders together with the invoicing and payment processing. These were deemed to be appropriate performance measures for the participating sample companies in the cluster. The performance of companies in the sample was likely to be indicative of the companies of the cluster and contributed to the knowledge and understanding of the cluster and its constituent firms. This knowledge and understanding provided input to the direction of future strategic interventions in the cluster. Table 7.4 presents the aggregate data for the whole sample of companies for the key performance measures.

**Table 7.4 – Performance measures for the sample companies**

| Performance Measure | Value |
|---|---|
| Value added per employee | 145923 |
| Stock turn | 34.8 |
| Production/Warehouse space | 2.1 |
| Warehouse/Total space | 0.3 |
| Ingredients/Turnover | 0.5 |
| Turnover per employee | 308461 |
| Average order value | 696 |
| Turnover per square m | 13514 |
| Turnover per square m production | 20079 |

The data presented here demonstrates that the values for turnover per employee and the value added per employee are very high when compared with other industry sectors. For example, the turnover per employee of over $300,000 is around twice that of many of the manufacturing companies, while the value added per employee of just under $150,000 is at least 50 per cent greater than that of comparable manufacturing companies. Table 7.5 presents the ranges of the values of performance measures.

**Table 7.5 – Ranges of performance measures for the sample companies**

| Performance Measure | Min | Max |
|---|---|---|
| Value added per employee | 37500 | 201465 |
| Stock turn | 8 | 128 |
| Production/Warehouse space | 0.7 | 2.0 |
| Warehouse/Total space | 0.17 | 0.77 |
| Ingredients/Turnover | 0.03 | 0.83 |
| Turnover per employee | 62500 | 642857 |
| Average order value | 70 | 43000 |
| Turnover per square m | 1417 | 12857 |
| Turnover per square m production | 2125 | 17307 |

Table 7.5 demonstrates the diversity of the companies in the sample with a factor of five separating the minimum and maximum value added per employee and a factor of 16 separating the lowest and highest stock turn. The value added per employee range relates to a small recently started firm at the lower end and a mature food processor with significant investment in plant, equipment and machinery. The latter range, the stock turn reflects the difference between the producer of a product that needs some considerable time to mature between production and sale, for example, cheese, compared to a fresh produce company where the time on the processor's premises is a few of days at most. There is similar diversity in the use of space by the very different industry producers. The difference for the turnover per employee between the minimum and maximum is

a factor of ten, which is a large disparity. The overall average order value figures indicate that the order values tend to be rather low, with a large number of orders to be filled. This is an indication that a significant amount of effort will be expended in the processing of order paperwork, accounts and associated administration. Clearly, some of this type of benchmarking would only be meaningful when industry participants with similar operating characteristics are involved in the comparisons. However, one conclusion from this data was that process benchmarking would be an appropriate next step for the administrative processes associated with order processing. The large number of transactions indicated that it would repay the effort to identify 'best practice' among cluster members in the area of order processing and administration. Other process benchmarking activity could be considered for subgroups of the cluster where the operational characteristics of the firms are similar.

## Migration and the development of food clusters in urbanised regions of China

The migration statistics for Australia, coupled with the census data that is collected periodically provides a valid and reliable basis for the analysis of the development of food processing, fusion cuisine and the food industry in Australia. The major waves of migration have been well documented and many of the food processing companies are now quite mature and passing through succession phases as a new generation assumes ownership and management of the enterprise.

By contrast, the situation in China is somewhat less clear, since the patterns of migration are predominantly internal to China. The complication that arises relates to the '*Hukou System*' which was introduced in cities in China in 1951 and extended to rural areas in 1955

(Song, Thisse and Zhu 2012). The Hukou system was originally used to manage and control the movement of people across boundaries from rural to urban or major city to major city. For example, the movement of urban residents within the same city or town is usually allowed, as is the movement of rural residents within their rural area. However, movements from small towns to large towns, towns to cities, or rural areas to urban areas are not usually permitted under the Hukou system. Consequently, under the Hukao system, people are regarded as being domiciled in their place of original residence unless they have been granted approval by the authorities, an approval that is only rarely granted (Song, Thisse and Zhu 2012).

The consequence of this system is that migration does take place, but it is difficult to quantify and track because official statistics, for example census data, do not reflect the existence of a large population of 'invisible residents'. These residents are regarded as a 'floating population' of temporary residents despite having been in their current location for years or even decades. Thus, in order to compute appropriate migration statistics that track migration patterns and allow inferences and comparisons to be made, it is necessary to derive the numbers from a variety of databases (Chan 2013).

The migration figures estimated using such approaches indicate that 'rural migrant labour' indicated that the figure was around 155 million people in 2010 (Chan 2013). The urbanisation over the period 1979 to 2009 in China resulted in growth of urban population of about 440 million to 622 million, made up of migration and reclassification of areas from rural to urban (Chan 2013). These numbers are sufficiently large to be able to infer that there is likely to have been significant development of food processing industries on the urban fringes of large Chinese towns and cities.

## Conclusion

The development of food clusters in regions with significant migrant communities has the potential to make significant contributions to the cuisine of the region through the development of an 'urban creative-food economy' (Donald and Blay-Palmer 2006) and the emergence of a vibrant SME sector food processing industry that incorporates specialty, local, ethnic and organic food processing (Donald and Blay-Palmer 2006). The urban market has responded with demand for 'high quality, local, fresh ethnic and fusion cuisines' (Donald and Blay-Palmer 2006). The structure of the SME food processing sector in Melbourne's North reflects the findings of the 'Toronto food cluster' that waves of migration have resulted in considerable enrichment in the availability and variety of foods and cuisines. The waves of migration from rural China to the urban manufacturing centres provides the context for significant enrichment of the urban Chinese food market as a result of the development of organic, ethnic and fusion cuisine alternatives. The capabilities of the Chinese entrepreneurial food processors will continue to ensure that these new markets are served by new enterprises that deliver what the consumers want. Once the majority of these urban creative food economy enterprises are in the mature phase of their development, which many of them are likely to be, they will require embarking on ongoing competitive improvement.

## Acknowledgement

The author acknowledges the support of the City of Whittlesea Council as part of the commitment to the food cluster in Northern Metropolitan Melbourne known as the Plenty Food Group. The support of participating companies is also acknowledged.

# References

Australian Bureau of Statistics (2014) 4102.0 – Australian Social Trends, 2014. http://www.abs.gov.au/ausstats/abs@.nsf/Lookup/4102.0main+features1 02014#MELBOURNE Viewed 20th August 2014.

Abor, J., & Quartey, P. (2010). Issues in SME development in Ghana and South Africa. *International Research Journal of Finance and Economics*, 39(6), 215-228.

Asheim, B. T., & Coenen, L. (2005). Knowledge bases and regional innovation systems: Comparing Nordic clusters. *Research policy*, 34(8), 1173-1190.

Avermaete, T., Viaene, J., Morgan, E. J., Pitts, E., Crawford, N., & Mahon, D. (2004). Determinants of product and process innovation in small food manufacturing firms. *Trends in Food Science & Technology*, 15(10), 474-483.

Bertolini, P., & Giovannetti, E. (2006). Industrial districts and internationalization: the case of the agri-food industry in Modena, Italy. *Entrepreneurship and regional development*, 18(4), 279-304.

Blay-Palmer, A., & Donald, B. (2006). A tale of three tomatoes: The new food economy in Toronto, Canada. *Economic Geography*, 82(4), 383-399.

Blundel, R. K., & Hingley, M. (2001). Exploring growth in vertical inter-firm relationships: small-medium firms supplying multiple food retailers. *Journal of Small Business and Enterprise Development*, 8(3), 245-265.

Ceglie, G., Clara, M., & Dini, M. (1999). *Cluster and network development projects in developing countries: lessons learned through the UNIDO experience. Boosting innovation the cluster approach*, 269.

Chan, K. W. (2008, January). *Internal labor migration in China: trends, geographical distribution and policies.* In Proceedings of the United Nations Expert Group Meeting on Population Distribution, Urbanization, Internal Migration and Development (pp. 93-122).

Chan, K. W. (2013). China: internal migration. *The Encyclopedia of Global Human Migration.*

DIBP, (2014). Department of Immigration and Border Protection Fact Sheet 4 – More than 65 Years of Post-war Migration http://www.immi.gov.au/media/fact-sheets/04fifty.htm#a accessed 20th August 2014.

Donald, B., & Blay-Palmer, A. (2006). The urban creative-food economy: producing food for the urban elite or social inclusion opportunity?. *Environment and planning A*, 38(10), 1901.

Gellynck, X., Vermeire, B., & Viaene, J. (2007). Innovation in food firms: contribution of regional networks within the international business context. *Entrepreneurship & Regional Development*, 19(3), 209-226.

Johnston, R. (2004). Clusters: a review of their basis and development in Australia. *Innovation: management, policy & practice*, 6(3), 380-391.

Karaev, A., Koh, S. L., & Szamosi, L. T. (2007). The cluster approach and SME competitiveness: a review. *Journal of Manufacturing Technology Management*, 18(7), 818-835.

North, D., & Smallbone, D. (2000). Innovative activity in SMEs and rural economic development: Some evidence from England. *European Planning Studies*, 8(1), 87-106.

Oyelaran-Oyeyinka, B. (2001). Networks and linkages in African manufacturing cluster: a Nigerian case study. *Networks*, 5.

Requier-Desjardins, D., Boucher, F., & Cerdan, C. (2003). Globalization, competitive advantages and the evolution of production systems: rural food processing and localized agri-food systems in Latin-American countries, *Entrepreneurship & Regional Development*, 15(1), 49-67.

Robertson, P. L., & Patel, P. R. (2007). New wine in old bottles: Technological diffusion in developed economies. *Research Policy*, 36(5), 708-721.

Saleh, A. S., & Ndubisi, N. O. (2006). An evaluation of SME development in Malaysia. *International Review of Business Research Papers*, 2(1), 1-14.

Song, H., Thisse, J. F., & Zhu, X. (2012). Urbanization and/or rural industrialization in China. *Regional Science and Urban Economics*, 42(1), 126-134.

Traill, B. (1997). Globalisation in the food industries?. *European Review of Agricultural Economics*, 24(3-4), 390-410.

Wilkinson, J. (2008). *The food processing industry, globalization and developing countries. The Transformation of Agri-Food Systems: Globalization, Supply Chains and Smallholder Farmers.* Food & Agriculture Org., New York, 87-108.

# Appendix

Program – Knowledge exchange of quality food production and distribution: China and Australia forum – 11-12 November 2013.

<table>
<tr><th colspan="2">KNOWLEDGE EXCHANGE OF QUALITY FOOD PRODUCTION AND DISTRIBUTION: CHINA AND AUSTRALIA FORUM (11-12 NOVEMBER)<br>Hosted by Huazhong Agricultural University (HZAU) In Partnership With Swinburne University of Technology (SUT)</th></tr>
<tr><th colspan="2">DAY ONE: MONDAY 11 NOVEMBER</th></tr>
<tr><th>Time</th><th>Event</th></tr>
<tr><td>4:00 pm-6:00 pm</td><td>Registration Opens</td></tr>
<tr><td>6:00pm-6:30pm</td><td>Welcome Address<br>• Professor Chongguang Li (Vice President of Huazhong Agricultural University)<br>• Professor Barry O'Mahony (Head of Marketing, Tourism and Social Impact; Swinburne University of Technology, Australia)</td></tr>
<tr><td>6:30pm-8:30pm</td><td>Dinner And Networking</td></tr>
<tr><th colspan="2">DAY TWO : TUESDAY 12 NOVEMBER</th></tr>
<tr><td>9:00am-09:30am</td><td>Welcome Plenary<br>• Australian Speaker: Mr Jeff Turner (Austrade) welcoming on behalf of Australian Government<br>• Chinese Speaker: to be confirmed on behalf of the Chinese Government<br>• Chinese Speaker: to be confirmed on behalf of Huazhong Agricultural University<br>Chair: Professor Ping Qing (Dean of Faculty of Business & Management, Huazhong Agricultural University)</td></tr>
</table>

<table>
<tr><td>9:30am-10:20am</td><td colspan="2">Topic: Agribusiness<br>Keynote Australian Speaker:<br>• Mr Jeff Turner (Australian Trade Commission)<br>• Mr Patrick Stringer (Victorian Government Commissioner)<br>Chinese Speaker:<br>• To Be Confirmed (TBC)<br>Chair: Associate Professor Bruno Mascitelli (Associate Dean International, Swinburne University of Technology, Australia)</td></tr>
<tr><td>10:20am-10:30am</td><td colspan="2">Group Photo Session</td></tr>
<tr><td>10:30am-11:00am</td><td colspan="2">MORNING TEA</td></tr>
<tr><td colspan="3">Parallel Sessions</td></tr>
<tr><td></td><td>ROOM A<br>(RED ROOM)<br>Co-chair: Professor Barry O'Mahony</td><td>ROOM B<br>(GREEN ROOM)<br>Co-chair: Associate Professor Bruno Mascitelli</td></tr>
<tr><td>11:00am-11:45am</td><td>Topic: Agritourism (Food & Wine)<br>Australian Speaker:<br>• Ms Nikki Palun (De Bortoli Wines Pty Ltd)<br>Chinese Speaker:<br>• TBC</td><td>Topic: Food Security<br>Australian Speaker:<br>• Dr Mark Gibson (Institute for Tourism Studies, Macao SAR China)<br>Chinese Speaker:<br>• TBC</td></tr>
</table>

| | | |
|---|---|---|
| 11:45am-12:30pm | **Topic: Agritourism (Food & Wine)**<br>Australian Speaker:<br>• Mr Gary Dick (William Angliss Institute)<br>Chinese Speaker:<br>• TBC | **Topic: Food Security & Agritourism**<br>Australian Speaker:<br>• Ms Cathy Yang (The Hong Kong Polytechnic University)<br>Chinese Speaker:<br>• TBC |
| 12:30pm- 2:00pm | **LUNCH** | |
| 2:00pm-2:45pm | **Topic: Gastronomy**<br>Australian Speaker:<br>• TBC (William Angliss Institute)<br>Chinese Speaker: | **Topic: Supply Chain Management**<br>Australian Speaker:<br>• Associate Professor Antonio Lobo (SUT)<br>Chinese Speaker: |
| 2:45pm-3:30pm | **Topic: Gastronomy**<br>Australian Speaker:<br>• Mr Tony Bilson (Bilson's Restaurant)<br>Chinese Speaker:<br>• TBC | **Topic: Logistics**<br>Australian Speaker:<br>• Dr Nicholas Grigoriou (Monash Sunway University Malaysia)<br>Chinese Speaker:<br>• TBC |
| 3:30pm-4:00pm | **AFTERNOON TEA** | |

| | | |
|---|---|---|
| 4:00pm-4:45pm | **Topic: Competitiveness**<br>Australian Speaker:<br>• Professor John Dalrymple (SUT)<br>Chinese Speaker:<br>• TBC | **Topic: Organic**<br>Australian Speaker:<br>• Dr John Paull (University of Tasmania)<br>Chinese Speaker:<br>• TBC |
| 4:45pm-5:30pm | **Topic: Dairy**<br>Australian Speaker:<br>• Mr Henry Hong (Bellamy's Organic Pty Ltd)<br>Chinese Speaker:<br>• TBC | **Topic: Organic**<br>Australian Speaker:<br>• Dr Jue Chen (SUT)<br>Chinese Speaker:<br>• TBC |
| 5:30 pm-6:00pm | **Forum Wrap Up and Conclusion:**<br>• Professor Chongguang Li (Vice President of HZAU)<br>• Professor Barry O'Mahony (Head of Marketing, Tourism and Social Impact - SUT) | |
| 6:00pm-7:00pm | **BREAK** | |
| 7:00pm-8:30pm | **DINNER AND NETWORKING**<br>Book Launch by Associate Professor Antonio Lobo | |

# Index

www.ingramcontent.com/pod-product-compliance
Lightning Source LLC
Chambersburg PA
CBHW071118280326
41935CB00010B/1047

* 9 7 8 1 9 2 5 1 3 8 3 9 9 *